The Maximizer Mindset

The Maximizer Mindset

Work Less, Achieve More, Spread Joy

Katie Alaniz and David Hao

ROWMAN & LITTLEFIELD
Lanham • Boulder • New York • London

Published by Rowman & Littlefield
An imprint of The Rowman & Littlefield Publishing Group, Inc.
4501 Forbes Boulevard, Suite 200, Lanham, Maryland 20706
www.rowman.com

86-90 Paul Street, London EC2A 4NE

British Library Cataloguing in Publication Information Available

Library of Congress Cataloging-in-Publication Data

Names: Alaniz, Katie, 1980- author. | Hao, David, 1985- author.
   Title: The maximizer mindset : work less, achieve more, spread joy / Katie
      Alaniz and David Hao.
   Description: Lanham. Maryland : Rowman & Littlefield, [2022] | Includes
      bibliographical references. | Summary: "Purpose and planning form the
      core of the Maximizer Mindset, designed to empower individuals within a
      myriad of contexts to work less, achieve more, and spread joy throughout
      each day of their lives"-- Provided by publisher.
   Identifiers: LCCN 2022012092 (print) | LCCN 2022012093 (ebook) | ISBN
      9781475863611 (Cloth) | ISBN 9781475863628 (Paperback
) | ISBN 9781475863635 (eBook)
   Subjects: LCSH: Happiness. | Time management. | Creative ability. | Goal
      (Psychology)
   Classification: LCC BF575.H27 A429 2022 (print) | LCC BF575.
   H27 (ebook) |
      DDC 158.1--dc23/eng/20220413
   LC record available at https://lccn.loc.gov/2022012092
   LC ebook record available at https://lccn.loc.gov/2022012093

Katie and David dedicate this book to the glory of God.

Additionally, Katie dedicates this book to her husband, Steven Alaniz, and parents, Bob and Belinda Ellis and Rey and Rose Alaniz, who consistently model the beauty of prioritizing purpose. These cherished individuals wholeheartedly devote their lives to the pursuit of blessing others.

David also dedicates this book to his amazing great-grandma-in-law and good buddy, Margaret "Mommog" Walp, the maximizer of maximizers. Mommog lived 106 amazing years of life and spread joy to countless people.

Contents

Preface

The inspiration for writing this guidebook developed as a result of numerous shared experiences. We, Katie Alaniz and David Hao, first met as colleagues at Houston Baptist University in Houston, Texas. Through our service at a faith-based institution of higher education and our work to enhance the lives of our students, we quickly learned that we share a joint passion for making the most of life through finding ways to add value to the lives of others. Although this mindset is not always easy to maintain, this is at the heart of our "why" for living.

Ultimately, our "why" resides in the mission to know Christ and to make Him known to others. As His followers, inspired by the fact that He "came not to be served but to serve . . . " (Matthew 20:28 NIV), we hold the joint belief that the most meaningful life experiences include service to others. The greatest leaders, in fact, are those willing to serve. Individuals who maintain a servant's heart place aside their own agenda in the pursuit of carrying out a mission aligned with Christ's mission—the mission to live a life of love. Jesus taught that " . . . whoever wants to become great among you must be your servant, and whoever wants to be first must be slave of all" (Mark 10:44 NIV). He called His followers to do the same.

This way of living stands in stark contrast to much of what we encounter daily in today's world. Most people will say or do nearly anything to stay a step ahead of others as they maneuver their way to the top of the ladder. Whether in academic settings, in professional settings, in political settings, or even in social and familial settings, so many individuals instinctively strive to work their way up to the top—sometimes at great expense to others within their spheres of influence.

Yet, from Christ's perspective, rank, titles, credentials, and possessions mean little in the scheme of life. This is because He came to serve and not to be served, taking our human conceptions of key rules of engagement and turning them upside down. He reminds us that in ordinary life occurrences, we witness God's extraordinary grace. To encounter miracles, we must be a miracle to others. When we give of our time, talent, and treasure to enrich the lives of others, our own lives will naturally be enriched.

The principle resides at the heart of the Maximizer Mindset, allowing individuals to achieve more while spreading increased light within the lives of others. We have found that as we focus less on the "to-dos" and more on the "why we do what we do," life begins to make better sense, and our days are filled with greater joy. We hope and pray that this will be true for you too, as you seek to embrace new ways to work less while achieving more and spreading greater joy. This is what the Maximizer Mindset is all about!

Acknowledgments

We, Katie and David,

would like to convey our deepest gratitude to our spouses,

Steven and Claire,

and to our families and friends

for wholeheartedly encouraging us

and faithfully offering prayers and wisdom

throughout our journeys to embrace our lives' purposes.

Introduction

In today's fast-paced world, many individuals unknowingly find themselves on a quest to win the race against time. The current digital age has overhauled how we interact with and conceptualize time, as constant streams of pressing notifications and packed schedules put tremendous stress on the minds of modern humankind. Now more than ever before, living a joyful and productive life requires intentional design. Purpose and planning form the core of the Maximizer Mindset, designed to empower individuals within a myriad of contexts to work less, achieve more, and spread joy throughout each day of their lives.

Chapter one begins by detailing the subtle ways in which the age of innovation has brought about a shortage of bandwidth and an abundance of burnout. The expansion of digital tools and resources designed to enhance productivity has also increased the typical pace of life, as well as the expectation that more should be accomplished in less time. Ever so slowly, society's perception of time has been altered. In a do-more culture, many find themselves unrealistically cramming as many activities as possible into their daily schedules. In doing so, they neglect planning with purpose.

All of us will eventually die, and this should ignite a sense of urgency within us—a sense of urgency arising from a key question: "When our days on earth are through, will we have maximized our time on what matters most?" This question is at the heart of the Maximizer Mindset, which will be explored more fully in the coming chapters.

Chapter two introduces the keys to unlocking the Maximizer Mindset, which include the following: 1) Find freedom by treasuring truth. 2) Ignite productivity by prioritizing purpose. 3) Cultivate creativity by leveraging connections.

The Maximizer Mindset empowers individuals in countless personal and professional contexts to work less, achieve more, and spread joy through embracing these three keys. This book deeply delves into providing research, narratives, and real-life applications of these principles.

A principle that stands the test of time is "the truth will set you free," or *Veritas liberabit vos* in the Greek. The English variation, "And You Shall Know the Truth and the Truth Shall Make You Free," is notably carved in stone on the Original Headquarters Building of the Central Intelligence Agency. This phrase, adopted as a motto by numerous universities and colleges, is both frequently stated yet often overlooked in today's world. In fact, it can be difficult to know what to believe in our modern society.

In a day in which "fake news" is a common buzzword, fabricated stories are presented as truth, and photoshopped lives are the norm, we find ourselves sorting fact from fiction on a daily basis. Chapter three tackles time-management myths that sometimes hinder us from finding freedom. Most importantly, it overviews truths to embrace about time and time management, which ultimately lay the foundation for the Maximizer Mindset.

It seems challenging to identify a concept that has garnered more interest in recent years than the growth mindset. This idea, based on the work of Stanford psychologist Carol Dweck, centers upon the theory that those who believe their abilities can be developed outperform those who believe their abilities are fixed. When misinterpreted, however, this thinking may have a negative impact upon growth and productivity.

In a day and age in which motivational quotes are endemic on social media and influencers from realms of sports and business tell us that hard work is the sole recipe for success in life, it is easy to overestimate the power of effort. While effort is a necessary ingredient, more is required.

Why is it that many people do not find success, even in spite of how hard they try? Chapter four focuses upon the value of prioritizing purpose before effort, ultimately unlocking the key to igniting impactful productivity.

King Solomon of Israel, who was widely regarded as the recipient of unparalleled wisdom, famously remarked, "Two are better than one, because they have a good return for their labor: If either of them falls down, one can help the other up. But pity anyone who falls and has no one to help them up."

As a statement often quoted at weddings, many assume that the principle "two are better" is relegated to marriage. However, this could not be farther from the truth. Although certainly applicable to the partnership within marriage, this principle applies to countless aspects of life.

In a world in which individualism is often prized, far too many overlook the power of connectivity. In fact, creativity flourishes through effective collaboration, but not all partnerships are created equal. Chapter five presents practical steps for discovering, developing, and capitalizing upon "perfect pairings" to cultivate creativity.

The Maximizer Mindset encourages and empowers individuals to add value to their lives and the lives of others. Those who embrace this mindset achieve freedom by seeking truth, spark productivity by prioritizing purpose, and promote creativity by leveraging connections. In doing so, they bring infinite value to various contexts of life, including family and social dynamics, professional spheres, and areas of service.

Additionally, they naturally inspire others in obtaining newfound freedom, gaining remarkable productivity, and unlocking powerful creativity as they work towards their own goals in life. Chapter six focuses upon the inherent, priceless result of unlocking the Maximizer Mindset, namely adding value to all areas of life.

Chapter seven provides the reader with opportunities to explore practical applications of the Maximizer Mindset that relate to every aspect of life. The Maximizer Mindset provides space to focus on winning in the areas of life that truly matter.

Individuals who embrace this mindset understand that giving it your all, all the time, is not what counts. In fact, this will likely result in frustration, burnout, failure, and alienation. Those who take on the Maximizer Mindset instead focus on substance before style, intentionally embracing purpose and the power of partnerships. This ultimately results in increased meaning and margin in life, as time is maximized on what matters most.

Chapter One

The Race Against Time

"It is not enough to be busy . . . The question is: what are we busy about?"

—Henry David Thoreau

In today's fast-paced world, many individuals unknowingly find themselves on a quest to win the race against time. The current digital age has overhauled how we interact with and conceptualize time, as constant streams of pressing notifications and packed schedules put tremendous stress on the minds of modern humankind.

Few facets of life in the industrialized world seem more undeniable than how busy we consistently seem to be. Increasing numbers of people appear overstretched with work, often leaving far less margin for family members and friends. The concept of life/work balance is an increasingly popular topic at professional conferences, within magazine articles, and in blog posts, while still remaining an elusive concept that so many struggle to grasp.

We might assume the explanation is clear: people naturally feel busier than ever before because there is simply more to do. However, this is an incorrect assumption. The total time spent working—regardless of paid or unpaid hours—has, in fact, not risen in North America or Europe over the past several decades.

The ESRC Centre for Time Use Research, a leading multidisciplinary research-focused organization at the UCL Institute of Education in University College London (UCL), specializes in gathering and analyzing time use data. In doing so, they explore time as it relates to various facets of life, including socialization, life/work balance, family dynamics, and so on.

Jonathan Gershuny of the Centre for Time Use Research explains, "The headline changes over the last 50 years are that women do a whole lot less unpaid work, and a whole lot more paid work, and men do quite a bit less paid work, and a whole lot more unpaid work." Even still, "the total amounts of work are pretty much exactly the same." Furthermore, some who claim to be the busiest may be overestimating the amount of time they devote to work (Burkeman, 2016, para. 2).

For the average individual in today's world, reading these statements likely evokes surprise and possibly even a bit of skepticism. Surely our society is busier than ever before, as so many seem to struggle on a daily basis to check their most pressing tasks off to-do lists. If the total amount of work truly is the same, why do we so often feel as though there is exponentially more work to accomplish? Part of the answer involves basic economics. As economies develop and incomes of many have grown over the years, time has morphed into a more valuable commodity. Every moment is priceless, and for many, this leads to heightened pressure to compress more work into each hour.

This paradigm shift from ages past also relates to the type of work that occupies the majority of the population's time. Although bygone days were characterized by greater involvement in professions such as farming and manufacturing, this is no longer the case in the industrialized world. While manual labor can be physically taxing, it also adheres to certain limitations. For example, farmers cannot harvest crops until they have ripened to a certain extent, and manufacturers cannot create physical products unless needed materials have been made available to them.

However, our management of time has completely shifted in an era of what time-management consultant Peter Drucker termed "knowledge work." Moreover, according to Tony Crabbe, author of the book *Busy: How to Thrive in a World of Too Much*, today's society operates within an "infinite world." The norm for countless individuals includes a consistent influx of new emails, a full calendar of meetings, an expansive list of new articles or books to read, and an ever-growing collection of new endeavors to pursue.

Drucker remarked, "Until we can manage time, we can manage nothing else." Although effective time management represents a key factor in leading a healthy, productive, purposeful, and joyful life, growing percentages of the population seem to struggle with this concept in spite of, and sometimes as a result of, new developments designed to help people achieve this very goal.

The advent of digital mobile technologies not only brought newfound convenience but also introduced the concept of checking more items off the to-do list from home, on the road, while working out, and even while on vacation. As it becomes increasingly feasible to accomplish more in less time, we feel greater pressure to do exactly that. In turn, we grow more likely to face burnout.

Twenty years ago, we could not have imagined that digital tools and resources would provide ways of accomplishing so much in so little time—from literally any location on earth with Wi-Fi or cellular connection. Yet, even in spite of these technological advancements, the fact remains that society is composed of finite humans with finite capabilities and energy—humans seeking to accomplish an infinite amount of work in a finite amount of time.

The pressure to "do it all" has become the norm. Even still, the fact remains that this is mathematically unattainable; there are simply not enough hours in each day. And, when a goal is consistently left unmet, this naturally leads to frustration. Ultimately, the age of innovation has brought about a shortage of bandwidth and an abundance of burnout. The expansion of digital tools and resources designed to enhance productivity has also increased the typical pace of life, as well as the expectation that more should be accomplished in less time.

Ever so slowly, society's perception of time has been altered. In a do-more culture, many find themselves unrealistically cramming as many activities as possible into their daily schedules. In doing so, they neglect planning with purpose. Gradually, being "busy" has become a status symbol, which is ridiculous considering the impacts this lifestyle renders upon a person's mental, emotional, and physical health.

Now more than ever before, to live a joyful and productive life requires intentional design. Purpose and planning form the core of the Maximizer Mindset, designed to empower individuals within a myriad of contexts to work less, achieve more, and spread joy throughout each day of their lives.

Although adopting a lifestyle of surviving rather than thriving seems to be the norm in today's world, this need not be the case. We must each ask ourselves, "Do I want to live life or have life live me?" Although most of us would naturally say we desire the former, so many of us eventually default to the latter.

FINDING YOUR "WHYS"

The Maximizer Mindset centers upon the significance of prioritizing what matters most in life. The core of this mindset involves finding our "whys" and key callings as individuals. The process of discovering our purpose, or the foundational "whys" in our lives, is an exhilarating journey. By the same token, it will also require some uncomfortable discoveries and truth telling—to ourselves.

In his timeless book entitled *The 7 Habits of Highly Effective People: Restoring the Character Ethic*, Stephen Covey (1989) expounds upon life principles that naturally translate to countless personal and professional undertakings. Among these philosophies, Habit 2 emphasizes the significance of beginning with the end in mind. This clever practice is at the heart of the Maximizer Mindset.

Wise people map out new journeys in life by first contemplating the destination. Yogi Berra, an American baseball player known for his witty remarks, once commented, "If you don't know where you're going, you'll end up someplace else." Along these same lines, Antoine de Saint-Exupéry, a French poet, journalist, and pioneering aviator, simply observed, "A goal without a plan is a wish." Without an end in mind, there is little point in starting the journey.

The concept of beginning with the end in mind aligns with Simon Sinek's (2011) now well-known principle, "Start with why." In his inspiring book entitled *Start with Why: How Great Leaders Inspire Everyone to Take Action*, Sinek (2011) maintains that even though many, if not most, organizations can effortlessly describe *what* they do, and while some can easily explain *how* they are exceptional or better, few organizations can distinctly communicate *why* they do what they do.

Sinek (2011) explains,

> Knowing your WHY is not the only way to be successful, but it is the only way to maintain a lasting success and have a greater blend of innovation and flexibility. When a WHY goes fuzzy, it becomes much more difficult to maintain the growth, loyalty and inspiration that helped drive

the original success. By difficult, I mean that manipulation rather than inspiration fast becomes the strategy of choice to motivate behavior. This is effective in the short term but comes at a high cost in the long term. (p. 50)

Human beings, like the organizations they create, find it much more challenging to maintain growth as people, loyalty toward their commitments, and inspiration in life when their "whys" become fuzzy. Rather than being inspired by pursuits that consume their time, they press on in their endeavors without passion. In the short term, they may be able to survive, but in the long term, there is a greater cost to pay.

THE HAZARDS OF THE HUSTLE CULTURE

Countless individuals in today's world live by the "rise and grind" mindset. In fact, some wear this philosophy as a badge of honor. They answer in the affirmative to questions such as the following:

- Do you hit the ground running as soon as your feet hit the ground each morning?
- Do you find yourself compulsively checking mobile devices, waiting for the next notification to appear so that you can reply in an instant?
- Has your coffee or energy drink budget skyrocketed as you need more and more caffeine to keep the ideas flowing?
- Do you frequently set short deadlines and secretly enjoy the thrill of barely squeaking in under these deadlines, with little to no time to spare?
- Do you find yourself grumbling about the lack of time you have, even though you often overload your schedule with more than is humanly possible to accomplish each day?

Individuals who answer yes to these questions may be members of a cultural phenomenon known as the hustle culture. For some, nonstop hustling symbolizes a significant part of their identity. As they pile their plates with excessive amounts of tasks to accomplish, they buy into the idea that they are set apart from the masses. They increasingly feel, and are sometimes even told by others, that they seem "superhuman," capable of doing it all.

For many, the hustle culture even carries a sense of glamour, as spending countless hours working and fighting burnout symbolize dedication on the job. Many equate being busy with being important. For victims of the hustle culture, being "always-on" seems desirable; it seems acceptable, if not expected, to push themselves to a breaking point during all waking hours of the day. They brag about not having breaks, not taking time for rest over the weekends, and not ever resting on vacation.

Unsurprisingly, though, countless studies demonstrate that members of the hustle culture ultimately pay the price for their habits in the long term. As mental and physical health begins to deteriorate and relationships are damaged, quality of life rapidly declines. Careers are cut short, and an earlier death even becomes more likely. At the end of the day, members of the hustle culture find that they have worked incredibly hard for something they do not actually want. But, far too often, they realize the consequences only after irreparable damage has been done, including burnout and burnt relationships.

Those driven by the hustle culture unknowingly surrender their power as people. They eventually morph into slaves to internal and external forces such as unreasonable deadlines, excessive work stresses, or pleasing those within their professional and personal spheres. They soon become so acclimated to functioning on autopilot that they are not aware of their environment or themselves. They find themselves hurrying from sunrise to well past sunset each day, anxiously laboring away on various projects, concerned they might not be able to meet the next deadline. In this state, their minds are far from present, instead fixated on future worries or past misgivings. These external and internal forces become unkind masters, eventually backfiring as they bring about needless worry and eventually complete burnout.

MOVING TOWARD A MAXIMIZER MINDSET

Any individual at any given point in their lives can be driven by the hustle culture. Operating from this perspective does not equate to uniqueness or value. In fact, living on autopilot is easy in a society that consistently emphasizes the value of hustle. Yet, when our personal well-being, and the well-being of those we love, begins to take priority over "rise and grind," we find ourselves positioned to transition from surviving to thriving. The Maximizer Mindset focuses on feasible steps toward thriving, allowing for more purposeful accomplishments with less work and more joy.

Those who operate from the Maximizer Mindset cultivate meaningful productivity. Rather than devoting single-minded concentration to finishing any given task at hand, they devote the majority of their time to purposeful, intentionally selected pursuits. They find themselves more joyfully embracing and pursuing new goals, rather than haphazardly tackling item after item on their to-do lists, simply for the sake of being able to claim one achievement after another before moving onto the next.

After realizing that there is no pressure to live up to the expectations of the hustle culture, those who have taken on the Maximizer Mindset find themselves breathing a little easier, walking a little taller, and moving forward with greater enthusiasm for life in each step. These Maximizers realize their identity is no longer tethered to unrealistic demands for self-achievement, and they find more time to savor each priceless moment life brings. Rather than viewing a lack of time as the enemy, they learn to treasure the seconds, minutes, hours, and days they are given, appreciating new means of maximizing each moment at their fingertips.

Those who adopt this lifestyle reap countless physical, mental, emotional, and spiritual rewards. Naturally, their heart and respiratory rates slow, their muscles relax, and their minds become more at peace and clear. Thoughts, decisions, and corresponding actions become more intentional and balanced. Sleep is deeper, immunity is strengthened, blood pressure is decreased, and an abiding sense of well-being is produced. Studies also demonstrate that calmer methods for handling professional duties lead to greater productivity over time, higher-quality end results, and heightened long-term success.

The coming chapters overview three keys to unlocking the Maximizer Mindset, namely

1. Find freedom by treasuring truth.
2. Ignite productivity by prioritizing purpose.

3. Cultivate creativity by leveraging connections.

All of us will eventually die, and this should ignite a sense of urgency within us—a sense of urgency arising from a key question: "When our days on earth are through, will we have maximized our time on what matters most?" This question is at the heart of the Maximizer Mindset, which will be explored more fully in the coming chapters.

LET THE ADVENTURE BEGIN!

Maximizers consistently remain mindful of their "whys," naturally identifying the destination before starting each journey. They learn to effectively create and implement sustainable, agile systems and rhythms. The first step in the journey involves delving into an honest conversation with oneself. The remainder of the chapter outlines questions for consideration, as well as space to jot down answers. These questions specifically address the most crucial "whys" in life, providing those who devote the time, thought, and energy to honestly answering them with the critical foundation upon which the Maximizer Mindset is built.

Each day contains exactly 1,440 minutes. A comparatively small investment of 15 to 30 minutes devoted to deeply, sincerely reflecting upon the questions and challenges below will undoubtedly reap lasting dividends, positively impacting countless areas of life and commencing the journey toward achieving the Maximizer Mindset. Let the adventure begin!

- What brings you the greatest joy in life? Without hesitation, what first comes to mind? This might be a noun (person, place, thing, or idea) or verb (action).

  _____

  _____

  _____

  _____

  _____

  _____

_____

_____

_____

_____

- What did your ten-year-old self love doing most? What did you love doing just for the fun of it, without rewards, pressure, or the need to impress anyone?

_____

_____

_____

_____

_____

_____

_____

_____

_____

_____

- If you knew you were going to die a year from today, what would you accomplish over the coming year?

_____

_____

_____

_____

_____

_____

_____

_____

_____

_____

- As morbid as it may seem, write your ideal eulogy. How do you want to be remembered, and what do you want your legacy to be?

_____

_____

_____

_____

_____

_____

_____

_____

_____

_____

_____

_____

_____

_____

_____

ESSENTIAL IDEAS TO REMEMBER

Those who maintain a Maximizer Mindset first invest the time, thought, and energy necessary for honest reflection. They carefully identify their "whys," pinpointing the final destination before starting each journey. They strategically design and execute workable, responsive systems and rhythms.

This chapter highlights the importance of taking time for the first step of the journey, namely a heartfelt conversation with oneself. The remainder of the book builds upon answers to these questions in the adventure to attain the Maximizer Mindset, ultimately leading to less work, greater achievement, and more joy.

REFERENCES

Burkeman, O. (2016, September 11). *Why you feel busy all the time (when you're actually not)*. Future. https://www.bbc.com/future/article/20160909-why-you-feel-busy-all-the-time-when-youre-actually-not.

Covey, S. R. (1989). *The 7 habits of highly effective people: Restoring the character ethic*. New York: Free Press.

Crabbe, T. (2015). *Busy: How to thrive in a world of too much*. New York: Grand Central Publishing.

Sinek, S. (2011). *Start with why*. Harlow, England: Penguin Books.

Chapter Two

The Keys to Unlocking
the Maximizer Mindset

*"Time management is an oxymoron. Time is beyond our control, and
the clock keeps ticking regardless of how we lead our lives. Priority
management is the answer to maximizing the time we have."*

—John C. Maxwell

The Maximizer Mindset empowers individuals in countless personal
and professional contexts to work less, achieve more, and spread joy
through embracing three keys, namely, (1) Find freedom by treasuring
truth, (2) Ignite productivity by prioritizing purpose, and (3) Cultivate
creativity by leveraging connections. Each of these keys will be introduced in this chapter and explored in greater depth in the chapters to
come. Understanding—and ultimately application—of these keys does
not actually entail principles of time management. Rather, this involves
priority management.

Time is a limited commodity; at the start of each new week, every
individual begins with an allotment of exactly 168 hours in which to
tackle the tasks at hand. Although some may possess more talent, intelligence, educational and professional achievements, or money than
others, no one holds a unique advantage over any other person when
it comes to time. No matter how clever, no person in the history of
humankind will ever cheat the reality that every individual is allotted 24
hours in each day, 168 hours in each week, and 8,736 hours in each year.

FIRST THINGS FIRST

Although we cannot alter the amount of time we have at our disposal, we can more effectively leverage the time we have to accomplish the goals most significant to us. This strategy entails more than simply managing time. Instead, this is where priority management comes into play. This closely aligns with Habit 3 in Stephen Covey's (1989) classic book *The 7 Habits of Highly Effective People: Restoring the Character Ethic*.

This habit, "Put First Things First," is discussed more fully in the book *First Things First* (Covey, Merrill, & Merrill, 1995) and speaks to the heart of priority management. This principle also ties into the "Big Rocks" metaphor explored in Covey's book. Simply stated, the big rocks in life represent essential priorities. They signify those objectives or projects that must be accomplished. They symbolize mission-critical goals rather than bulleted items on a meandering to-do list.

The following "big rocks" analogy is relayed in *First Things First* (Covey, Merrill, & Merrill, 1995):

> *A time management expert was addressing a group of students, and he utilized an unforgettable illustration when speaking to them about priority management.*
>
> *He held up a one-gallon, wide-mouthed Mason jar and placed it on a table in front of him. Next, he displayed six fist-sized rocks and gently placed them into the Mason jar, one-by-one.*
>
> *Once he had filled the jar to the brim and no additional rocks would fit, he asked the class, "Would you say this jar is full?"*
>
> *Simultaneously, the students replied, "Yes."*
>
> *He asked, "Really?"*
>
> *From under the table, he then produced a bag of gravel. He gradually started pouring the gravel into the jar, periodically shaking the jar throughout this process in order that the gravel would fall into the spaces separating each of the larger rocks. He next smiled and questioned the group one more time, "Would you say this jar is now full?"*
>
> *Some of the students began to pick up on the lecturer's point. "Probably not," one of the students commented.*
>
> *"Great!" he responded. He then pulled a bag of sand from under the table. He began shaking the sand into the jar, and the grains of sand eventually sifted down, filling the spaces remaining amidst the gravel and rocks. Once more, he asked, " Would you say this jar is now full?"*

"No!" the students exclaimed.

"Wonderful!" he remarked, and he finally lifted a pitcher of water from the desk in front of him and began to pouring the water into the jar, until it was filled to the top.

He then asked the class, "What would you say is the point of this analogy?"

One student raised her hand and suggested, "The point of your analogy is that no matter how filled your schedule seems, with thought and effort, you will eventually be able to fit more within it!"

"Excellent try," the presenter replied, "but that is not actually the point. The truth this illustration reveals is simple yet profound: Unless the big rocks are placed in first, you will never be able to fit the rest in."

Although many understand and even wholeheartedly agree with the principle demonstrated by this illustration, few actually manage their time in ways that reflect this principle. Why does effective priority management seem like an illusive goal to so many?

Although the process of identifying priorities may appear intuitive, many individuals face the following three challenges as they seek to do so:

1. They possess an abundance of priorities.
2. They seem unable to decipher the truly vital priorities.
3. They allow less critical to-do items to prevent them from giving attention to what actually aligns with their more significant goals.

THE MOST IMPORTANT THING

Interestingly, the word "priority" appeared in the English language through way of Old French within the fourteenth century. It is derived from the medieval Latin word *prioritas*, which means "fact or condition of being prior." This word initially meant "the most important thing." When it first came into being, the word "priority" was without a plural form. Thus, one could maintain only one priority.

In the mid-twentieth century, the plural form of the words, "priorities," began to be utilized, likely as a result of the growth of corporate culture. The notion of having more than a single "most important thing" became more and more common. In fact, it no longer seemed unusual to formulate five, ten, fifteen, or more priorities. In reality, though, a person who has fifteen priorities truly is without priorities. It seems unlikely that a person or organization can remain mindful of an abundant collection of priorities, let alone actually prioritize them.

Effective prioritization involves a limited number of goals, and it requires an intentional, consistent focus of time, talent, and treasure on reaching these goals—while simultaneously avoiding the temptation to devote oneself to less significant pursuits.

"The oldest, shortest words—'yes' and 'no'—are those which require the most thought," Pythagoras remarked.

Ernest Agyemang Yeboah, a gifted Ghanaian writer and teacher, extended this thought, commenting, "It takes true courage and real humility to say no."

Why does it sometimes seem tremendously challenging to say "no" to new opportunities—even opportunities that seem promising but also may not align with set priorities? For some, the idea of saying "no" carries a fear of disconnection. It may seem that turning down a new opportunity will likely break bonds of connection with others—connections essential to our survival as human beings.

The thought of saying "no" may also bring about fear of causing another person to feel rejected. This may result in guilt or even embarrassment. Thus, the temptation to say "yes," even when this "yes" does not align with our priorities or interests—even when this "yes" does not feasibly fit within our schedules—becomes greater than the courage to say "no."

The struggle between whether to say "yes" or "no" also involves our own self-image. Each of us formulates a personal catalog of characteristics that collectively make up our self-image—characteristics such as "I am a giving person," "I willingly lend a hand to those in need," "I am unselfish with my time." Denying a request from another person calls these characteristics—and thus our own self-image—into question.

Yet, while the tendency to say "yes" too often may help us avoid temporary discomfort, we will eventually pay a long-term toll. Rather than safeguarding relationships, the habit of agreeing to do too much may eventually bring about resentment. This may also ultimately lead to burnout.

When the fear of how others may respond tempts us from saying "no" when a "yes" will not ultimately align with our priorities, we must remember that human beings often naturally maintain a harshness bias. In other words, we tend to assume that others will judge us much more critically than they do in reality. In fact, most people ultimately respect someone who exhibits the courage to say "no" when "yes" might fall outside of that person's priorities.

Warren Buffett once remarked, "The ability to say no is a tremendous advantage for an investor." While this quote might naturally bring about thoughts of wise financial investment practices, this principle also applies to the wise investment of time. Just as sage financiers do not make investment decisions as a result of fear or guilt, sage investors of time align their decisions with their priorities.

THE COMPOUNDED TIME CONUNDRUM

Effective priority management involves deeply considering key questions as we make choices regarding time. Such questions include, "If I replicated this decision each day for the next thirty years, would I appreciate the outcome?" For example, "If I skipped my workout, avoided professional development opportunities, held off on starting the book I've always wanted to write, and so on for the next thirty years, how would I feel about the consequences of this decision?"

Priority management requires innovative thinking regarding the investment of time on personally significant goals. This necessitates energy and thought devoted to outlining mission-critical goals. This means that priorities must be carefully selected, thus replacing the commonplace practice of categorizing every to-do as a priority. Effort that cannot be sustained over time will not align with the power of compound time. Attempting to accomplish too many perceived priorities over ten, twenty, or thirty years will result in fruitless efforts lacking a compounded impact. Ultimately, watered down results will emerge.

The passage of time, whether we realize it, multiplies both our actions as well as our inaction. Event still, this invisible force is often overlooked as individuals busy themselves with tasks to be accomplished on any given day. One example aligns with our daily eating habits. If a person consumes 3,000 calories per day while their body requires only 1,500 calories, over the course of a month, they will have ingested 46,500 extra calories. If this habit continues, within a year, they will have consumed an additional 558,000 calories. It is not hard to imagine how the results of this daily habit, compounded over a month and especially over a year, may begin to literally weigh a person down.

Compounded time impacts us in negative as well as positive ways. By leveraging the principle of compounded time along with clarity regarding essential priorities, we position ourselves to more effectively maximize time. Thus, we find ourselves empowered to tackle more that is important to us.

WHAT IS YOUR MISSION?

An essential component of priority management involves the development of a personal mission statement. Mission statements abound in today's world, from the "About Us" section of countless websites to the walls of company lobbies to the top paragraph of marketing brochures. Effective mission statements describe an organization's core identity and primary purpose, supporting organizational leaders in vision casting for the future.

However, mission statements are not limited to organizations. Personal mission statements, when efficaciously developed and implemented, hold the potential to profoundly impact the trajectory of life. They support individuals in recognizing significant goals and stirring up the intrinsic motivation to achieve these goals.

Whether a business executive, public servant, university student, stay-at-home parent, or whatever the professional calling, the process of designing a personal mission statement reaps great rewards. Developing and implementing a personal mission statement provides guidance and focus along the journey to achieve long-term goals. A personal mission statement provides a path to prevent wandering aimlessly in the adventure of life. For example, if a particular decision does not fit well within the confines of a personal mission statement, there is freedom not to follow through with this plan.

Individuals sometimes fail in their efforts to achieve goals due to a lack of clear focus. Without a mission to provide boundaries, it may be tempting to follow rabbit trails and ultimately experience a lost sense of purpose. On the other hand, successful people maintain solid focus on their personal mission statements. The questions included at the conclusion of this chapter are intended to guide readers through the process of designing a personal mission statement.

Through the process of crafting a personal mission statement, it is important to reflect upon key life principles and goals. Along this journey, several key questions to consider include: "Why did I set these goals?" and "How do these goals make me a better person?" A personal mission statement should address these essential questions in fifty words or less, avoiding the inclusion of unessential details.

There is no time like the present to begin writing a personal mission statement! This statement will impact each individual's intentional applications of the three keys to the Maximizer Mindset. Below are several examples of personal mission statements developed by well-known organizational leaders:

"To bring joy and happiness to other people." —Walt Disney

"To do more than survive, but to grow and live with passion, while meeting life with compassion, humor, and style." —Maya Angelou

"If something means enough to you, it should be pursued, even if you're likely to fail." —Elon Musk

"To have fun in [my] journey through life and learn from [my] mistakes." —Sir Richard Branson

"To use my gifts of intelligence, charisma, and serial optimism to cultivate the self-worth and net-worth of women around the world." —Amanda Steinberg

The following are several other mission statements from various corporations and nonprofit organizations:

"To accelerate the world's transition to sustainable energy." —Tesla

"Bring inspiration and innovation to every athlete* in the world. *If you have a body, you are an athlete." —Nike

"Style shouldn't break the bank." —MVMT

"To offer designer eyewear at a revolutionary price, while leading the way for socially conscious businesses." —Warby Parker

"Make commerce better for everyone, so businesses can focus on what they do best: building and selling their products." —Shopify

"Build the best product, cause no unnecessary harm, use business to inspire and implement solutions to the environmental crisis." —Patagonia

"To create a better everyday life for the many people." —IKEA

"Spread ideas." —TED

"To be Earth's most customer-centric company, where customers can find and discover anything they might want to buy online." —Amazon

"To become the world's most loved, most flown, and most profitable airline." —Southwest Airlines

"To organize the world's information and make it universally accessible and useful." —Google

"Become the world's number-one destination for fashion-loving 20-somethings." —ASOS

"To provide the best in cosmetics innovation to women and men around the world with respect for their diversity." —L'Oréal

"Help people perform better, think faster, and live better." —Bulletproof

"Create and promote great-tasting, healthy, organic beverages." —Honest Tea

"To inspire and nurture the human spirit—one person, one cup, and one neighborhood at a time." —Starbucks

"Our mission is to empower every person and every organization on the planet to achieve more." —Microsoft

"To give customers the most compelling shopping experience possible." —Nordstrom

"Squarespace empowers people with creative ideas to succeed. —Squarespace

"We ignite opportunity by setting the world in motion." —Uber

"To help bring creative projects to life." —Kickstarter

"To refresh the world in mind, body, and spirit. To inspire moments of optimism and happiness through our brands and actions." —The Coca-Cola Company

"To enable economic growth through infrastructure and energy development, and to provide solutions that support communities and protect the planet." —Caterpillar

"To nourish people and the planet. We're a purpose-driven company that aims to set the standards of excellence for food retailers. Quality is a state of mind at Whole Foods Market." —Whole Foods Market

"To spread the power of optimism." —Life Is Good

"The mission of LinkedIn is simple: connect the world's professionals to make them more productive and successful." —LinkedIn

"Our mission is to unlock the potential of human creativity—by giving a million creative artists the opportunity to live off their art and billions of fans the opportunity to enjoy and be inspired by it." —Spotify

"To entertain, inform, and inspire people around the globe through the power of unparalleled storytelling; reflecting the iconic brands, creative minds, and innovative technologies that make ours the world's premier entertainment company." —Disney

"To give people the power to build community and bring the world closer together." —Facebook

"To provide the best customer service possible. Deliver WOW through service." —Zappos

"The American Red Cross prevents and alleviates human suffering in the face of emergencies by mobilizing the power of volunteers and the generosity of donors." —The American Red Cross

"To inspire hope and contribute to health and well-being by providing the best care to every patient through integrated clinical practice, education, and research." —Mayo Clinic

"Seeking to put God's love into action, Habitat for Humanity brings people together to build homes, communities, and hope." —Habitat for Humanity

"To create content that educates, informs, and inspires." —Public Broadcasting System (PBS)

The following list provides fifty examples of personal mission statements (with the core statements encapsulated in the first sentence) and explanations of these mission statements included as well (Gaille, 2021, para. 4–54):

1. "To increase the net-worth of women so that they can achieve financial dependence and free themselves from crippling debt. To show these women how to wisely invest their money and get maximum returns. To help them become millionaires. I'd also like to have a positive impact on the lives of young girls by teaching them how to properly manage their money . . . "

2. "To provide the highest quality of customer service seen in my industry. By doing this, I will build a tribe of fanatical customers and buyers. These people will stay loyal to my business and help me become an industry leader. I'd also like to give back to the people who helped me along the way . . . "

3. "To repair the damage I have done to family members through my actions. To build real relationships and deeper connections with these people. To make up for the mistakes of the past and apologize for what I have done. In addition to this, I'd also like to reach out to people in my community and forge closer ties with them. Finally, I'd like to assist with various charities and community development projects in my area . . . "

4. "To use my gifts of intelligence for the benefit and improvement of others. To make use of the wisdom, knowledge, and logical thinking capabilities which God has given me. To put these skills into action and find a way to do good in the world. To assist others in overcoming burdens and reaching their true potential . . . "

5. "The purpose of this personal statement is to bring balance to my life. My biggest goal right now is to live a balanced life where I can maintain equilibrium between work, play, and friendship. I'd like to stop existing for work and living only for the weekend.

Instead, I want to live a stress-free life where I have enough time to relax and pursue my personal goals. By doing this, I also hope to improve my health, vitality, and spiritual well-being . . . "

6. "I work in an industry which is known for its dishonest[y]. The goal of my own mission statement is to remind myself that we need to do better. To this end, I'd like to begin by implementing ethical principles in my professional life. I'd like to learn how to operate from a position of total honest[y] and truthfulness. By doing this, I hope to reform this industry and encourage others to do the same . . . "

7. "I want to be a more courageous, outgoing, and positive person. The type of person who always looks on the bright side and sees the glass as half full. The type of person who lives life in a state of serial optimism and truly believes that the best is yet to come! I want to become someone who only thinks positively. I'd like to free myself from the shackles of the past!"

8. "My goal is to become the world leader in sustainable energy. I want to build a Fortune 500 company that heals instead of hurts the planet. By doing this, I hope to play a major role in the fight against global warming and climate change. It is my hope that our company will serve as a beacon of hope for people around the world. I want to show them that anything is possible if enough people come together to change things. My goal is to achieve all this by 2030 . . . "

9. "To become a social media maven and gain 100 million followers across all accounts. I want to become the world's first social media billionaire. When people think of social media, I want them to think of me. Once this is achieved, I'd like to convert this following into mainstream fame. My ultimate goal is to launch a global brand that becomes a household name. I dedicate myself to working non-stop until this goal is achieved . . . "

10. "I want to reach a deeper level of spirituality and inner peace. To find the guiding light which leads towards my North star. To live in harmony and grace with mother nature and with everything and everyone around me. To remain grounded and remind myself how lucky I am. To move into deeper and deeper levels of spiritual bliss. To show others how to do the same and achieve their own goals of gratitude and stillness . . . "

11. "To achieve my own personal definition of success and avoid backsliding into old and harmful behaviors. My idea of personal success is something I have yet to discover. At the moment, my goal is simply to continue my journey through life until I find something which inspires me. The goal when doing this is to maintain a healthy lifestyle. I'd also like to learn how to maintain healthy boundaries with other people. Especially those who would seek to harm or control me . . . "

12. "I'd like to become one of the most famous and renowned scientists in my field. To achieve this goal, I will do my best to help people through the application of science and technology. By doing this, I will create a better world for all mankind. Hopefully, this will bring me to the attention of my peers, and one day I will win a Nobel Prize for my efforts. Towards the end of my career, I'd like to give back by entering a teaching position. I will do this at a college like Harvard or Oxford . . . "

13. "I want to become the world's highest-paid personal development coach and eclipse the career of Stephen R. Covey. I want to become the next Tony Robbins and be as equally famous, rich, and successful. To do this, I will create the world's most sophisticated personal development programs. Along with this, I will become a master of sales, marketing, and advertising. Using these skills, I will sell millions of dollars of my products . . . "

14. "My ultimate purpose is to become the top life insurance salesman in my state. The reason why I want to do this is so that I can reap the financial rewards. In order to achieve this goal, I will sell more policies than anyone in my area and provide superior customer service. I will wake up every day with a plan for my work and schedule every minute of the day. I am prepared to work seven days a week if that's what it takes. I will never accept 'no' for an answer and keep pushing until the deal is closed . . . "

15. "My personal mission is to enhance the lives of others by making the world a better place. I truly believe that the attainment of world peace is possible in our lifetimes. The reason why there is strife, war, and discord is simply because people are struggling. All over the world, billions of people are living in desperate poverty. The key to changing the world is simply to help these people.

By dedicating my life to charity work, I will create a measurable difference in their lives . . . "

16. "My biggest goal in life is to develop my own personal brand. With this brand, I will create a business that generates more than 10 million dollars per year in revenue. The reason why I want to earn this type of money is so that I can enjoy the good life. You only live once, and I'd like to travel the world, eat good food, and experience the best that life has to offer . . . "

17. "To create a truly customer-centric company that provides the best customer service possible. My experience in the service industry has taught me that very few businesses provide true and honest customer service. Most customers are treated as an irritation. Businesses are only interested in the customers' money. I feel that by changing this, I can place myself ahead of the competition and build a million-dollar company . . . "

18. "To become the best version of myself and overcome the personal challenges I face right now. I'd like to stop living a life in which I manifest the worst possible version of myself. I want to see and experience everything of which I am truly capable of. I want to overcome the negative habits and thought patterns that are holding me back. Only by doing this can I become the person I was always meant to be . . . "

19. "To always make the right decision and thereby live a better everyday life. My biggest problem in life is that I am far too sloppy when it comes to decision-making. This has to change right now. I am going to become the type of person who can make the best decision every time. Not only that, I want to learn how to do this in only a few seconds—the reason why is because I am sick to death of putting off difficult choices. I want to learn how to make the right decisions. I am also sick of my endless procrastination . . . "

20. "To achieve my ultimate goals and do great things with my life. I have always been a highly ambitious person who chases after goals. I want to achieve more than other people have ever dreamt of. I know I can do this. It's simply a matter of persisting and putting my mind to it!"

21. "My greatest desire is to overcome burnout. I need to start managing my work-life balance. My main reason for doing this is

because I want to pursue my own goals outside of company time. My other goal is to work hard towards removing the sources of stress in my life. Eventually, I'd like to reach a point where I am almost entirely free of stress and worry . . . "

22. "My personal vision statement emphasizes the importance of doing the right things at the right time. I feel that the biggest reason why people fail is poor decision-making. Difficult decisions are put off or otherwise made too quickly. My goal is to avoid this and do exactly what needs to be done, exactly when it needs to be done. This is something which is often seen in a company vision statement, and with this philosophy, I will lead a better life and achieve my goals . . . "

23. "My personal vision statement involves following the trail of successful people in order to achieve my highest personal goals. I believe that success leaves clues. The key to becoming successful is simply to follow these clues. To this end, I will study the lives of successful people and implement the lessons they impart. This way, I can achieve the best probable outcome. By doing this, I hope to follow in their footsteps . . . "

24. "My own personal mission statement revolves around building habits through discipline. This way, I can achieve my long- and short-term goals. My personal belief is that we are the sum of our habits. The attainment of personal success relies upon creating these habits. It's possible to do anything as long as you have the right habits. I will work every day to build the habits needed for success . . . "

25. "To advance along my career path as quickly as possible. My deepest desire is to reach the CEO position before the age of 40. I believe this goal is attainable. This is true, no matter how impossible it may seem today. As long as I work hard and continue to improve myself, there's no reason why it shouldn't happen . . . "

26. "To live my life according to the following questions: What is right? What is honest? What is true? Too many people are liars without a moral compass. This is especially true in today's society. My mission is to be different. I'd like to strive for honesty and truth in all of my dealings, which is why I live my life according to these questions . . . "

27. "To find the fastest and best way to complete the task at hand. I believe that efficiency is the key to success. Those who work more efficiently are able to do more and thus achieve more. My goal is to find ways to continuously improve efficiency. This way, I will become the top performer in my workplace. By doing this, I will also rapidly rise through the ranks . . . "

28. "To create positive change for my clients and help them improve the hiring process. Too many companies fail because they hire the wrong people. I'd like to put a stop to this and help these companies succeed. I will do this in my capacity as a recruitment expert and consultant . . . "

29. "To be the team member who contributes the most to this organization. My goal is to ascend the career ladder as fast as possible. In order to achieve this, I will become the most valuable person in this organization. I will do this by offering the greatest contribution to this company and becoming an indispensable employee. When important decisions need to be made, the team will come to me . . . "

30. "To make a significant difference in the lives of inner-city school children by working tirelessly to improve their literacy rates. I'd like to dedicate my life to combatting this little-known problem. Too many inner-city kids are being pushed through school without even knowing how to read. This is something which we cannot allow to continue. My goal in life is to put a stop to this . . . "

31. "This year, I will dedicate myself to finally losing weight. I will eat right on a daily basis. By doing this, I will gradually lose weight and eventually reach my fitness goals. I will also dedicate myself to daily exercise. I will never skip a day and do whatever it takes to make this a reality. I will also work on my mindset by continually motivating myself with positive affirmations and thinking . . . "

32. "To stay focused and follow my long-term life goals so that I may achieve maximum satisfaction. For too many years, I have drifted mindlessly without an actual plan for life. This has led to substandard results, which I am no longer happy with. From now on, I will create actual goals. I will also break these down into daily, weekly, monthly, and yearly milestones . . . "

33. "My goal is to build New York's most prestigious creative agency. After years in this field, I've come to understand that good ideas are the foundation of this business. This is why my primary task from now on is to generate these ideas. I will spend at least an hour per day working on this. I will do whatever it takes to increase my creative abilities. I will do whatever it takes to come up with innovative concepts. Only by following this plan can my agency grow and retain high-value clients . . . "

34. "My greatest dream in life is to build a profitable low-cost airline. To do this, I will follow the exact same mission of Southwest Airlines and create a similar company vision statement. This is essentially to provide the best value for money, and to emphasize customer happiness and satisfaction. I will achieve this by training staff to the highest standards possible. This mission also includes actually listening to customers. This way, I can continually improve my service and stay ahead of the competition . . . "

35. "To discover the one great idea which can forever alter my business career and also improve the lives of others. I believe that the ultimate shortcut to success is finding one life-changing idea. By doing this, I could potentially become a millionaire overnight. My entire life will be consumed by discovering this. I refuse to give up until it happens . . . "

36. "My vision is to continuously move forward instead of focusing on things which hold me back. For too long, I have dwelt on past mistakes. Starting today, I will no longer live like this. Instead, I will set my sails in the right direction and only do things that benefit me. I will think positively. As long as I can stick to this, success is guaranteed . . . "

37. "To stop wasting so much time on video games and put work first. My career and relationships have suffered due to this addiction. From now on, I will limit myself to seven hours per week. Although this may be difficult at first, the stakes are too great. Unless I am able to overcome this problem, I will never live life to its fullest. By the end of this year, I hope to be completely free of video games . . . "

38. "To stay true to my most important values and beliefs so that I might maintain my personal integrity. I will strive to protect the things I hold most valuable. No matter what, I will never sacrifice

my honesty, integrity, or values. I will maintain this level of commitment regardless of how difficult it becomes, or however long the journey may take . . . "

39. "To develop the specific behaviors which will lead me to success. Over time I will discover these behaviors and practice them until they are hard-wired into my psyche. These include values such as goal setting, self-discipline, and hard work. I will do what it takes to become a better person. By doing this, life becomes easy. What's more, my success is almost assured . . . "

40. "To sort out my personal life and put more focus on my career and goals. From now on, I will never make the same mistake twice. I will stop spending time with negative people. Instead, I will surround myself with positivity and use this energy to create the life I've always deserved. Although this may take hard work, I am more than willing to put in the time, effort, and sacrifice . . . "

41. "To stop putting off big decisions and be more proactive when it comes to my career decisions. I will no longer procrastinate and avoid what needs to be done. Instead, I will act proactively and take charge of my career. I will no longer rely on other people to give me handouts. I will make things happen for myself. I will do whatever it takes to pursue my destiny and reach the apex of my industry . . . "

42. "To always put the first step first. To do this instead of worrying about the next, or about what could happen. I will remove all negative emotions which hold me back. Any action which causes fear, doubt, or stress will be eliminated. I will focus exclusively on positive actions which create positive emotions. With these actions, I will generate the psychic energy needed to achieve my wishes. I will live a life that is happier, more fulfilled, and less unstable. I will make this a reality for myself . . . "

43. "I believe that knowledge is power. I also believe that world-changing information is mostly inaccessible to the masses. The goal of my life is to remedy this. I want to make information freely available to anyone. No matter where they are in the world. I will do this by creating one easy-to-use and access directory. With this directory, I can begin to store the world's information and bring it to the masses . . . "

44. "To stay true to my own personal vision and quit spending so much time chasing other people's dreams. My goal in life is to start focusing on my own dreams. I want to stop helping other people achieve their goals while ignoring my own. I will do this by learning how to say no to people. I will do this by increasing my self-esteem and confidence. This may be difficult at first, but if I persist, it will become easier . . . "

45. "I want to find a great way to save significant time on the tax return process. I want to make filing taxes effortless. I want to find a way to make taxes easier for everyone. The reason why I want to do this is because I genuinely have a desire to help people. I've seen first-hand what people go through during tax time. I'd like to put a stop to this suffering . . . "

46. "I want to become a highly successful social media influencer and vlogger. I know that in order to do this, I have to be bigger and better than everyone else. I will achieve this goal by having the type of life experiences which make other people jealous . . . "

47. "My goal is to become Chicago's highest-paid business insider. I want to become the most knowledgeable person when it comes to local business. The purpose of doing this is so that I can become the city's most popular business consultant. By having insider knowledge, I am sure to attract the region's most valuable consulting clients . . . "

48. "My goal in life is to become one of the world's highest-paid SEO experts. I will do this by developing a great tool for SEO that saves time, money, and effort. My mission is to create the next generation of SEO tools and that these will be used by millions of people. Along with this, I will build one of the biggest SEO service companies in the world. I will also create a corporate mission statement which imparts these values to my staff . . . "

49. "To continually search for the next step so that I can burst through the barriers which are holding me back. To find new and innovative ways of doing things. To strive for innovation in the workplace. To be an idea generator who other people look to for inspiration. To come up with new and insightful ways of doing things . . . "

50. "My own statement for personal success is this: the only way to get what you want is by helping others get what they want. The

bottom line is that those who are genuinely willing to help will never struggle. Every person you help will one day help you . . . "

THE THREE KEYS TO THE MAXIMIZER MINDSET

The process of devoting time and careful reflection to developing a personal mission statement provides a solid foundation for embarking upon the three keys to the Maximizer Mindset. These principles are briefly overviewed in this chapter and explored in greater depth within the remainder of the book.

Maximizer Key 1: Find Freedom by Treasuring Truth

A principle that stands the test of time is "The truth will set you free," or *Veritas liberabit vos* in the Greek. The English variation, "And you shall know the truth and the truth shall make you free," is notably carved in stone on the Original Headquarters Building of the Central Intelligence Agency (CIA). This phrase, adopted as a motto by numerous universities and colleges, is both frequently stated and often overlooked in today's world. In fact, it can be difficult to know what to believe in our modern society.

Chapter three tackles time management myths that sometimes hinder us from finding freedom. Most importantly, it overviews truths to embrace about time and time management, which ultimately lay the foundation for the Maximizer Mindset.

Maximizer Key 2: Ignite Productivity by Prioritizing Purpose

It seems challenging to identify a concept that has garnered more interest in recent years than the growth mindset. This idea, based on the work of Stanford psychologist Carol Dweck, centers upon the theory that those who believe their abilities can be developed outperform those who believe their abilities are fixed. When misinterpreted, however, this thinking may have a negative impact upon growth and productivity.

In a day and age in which motivational quotes are endemic on social media and influencers from realms of sports and business tell us that hard work is the sole recipe for success in life, it is easy to overestimate the power of effort. While effort is a necessary ingredient, more is required.

Why is it that many people do not find success in spite of how hard they try? Chapter four focuses upon the value of prioritizing purpose before effort, ultimately unlocking the key to igniting impactful productivity.

Maximizer Key 3: Cultivate Creativity by Leveraging Connections

King Solomon of Israel, who was widely regarded as the recipient of unparalleled wisdom, famously remarked, "Two are better than one, because they have a good return for their labor: If either of them falls down, one can help the other up. But pity anyone who falls and has no one to help them up."

As a statement often quoted at weddings, many assume that the principle "two are better" is relegated to marriage. However, this could not be farther from the truth. Although certainly applicable to the partnership within marriage, this principle applies to countless aspects of life.

In a world in which individualism is often prized, far too many overlook the power of connectivity. In fact, creativity flourishes through effective collaboration, but not all partnerships are created equal. This chapter presents practical steps for discovering, developing, and capitalizing upon "perfect pairings" to cultivate creativity.

Each day contains exactly 1,440 minutes. A comparatively small investment of 15 to 30 minutes devoted to deeply, sincerely reflecting upon the questions and challenges below will undoubtedly reap lasting dividends, positively impacting countless areas of life and commencing the journey toward achieving the Maximizer Mindset. Priority management begins now!

- What do you consider to be your top five skills and abilities? What do you *really* like to do?

  _____

  _____

  _____

  _____

  _____

_____
_____
_____
_____
_____

• What five characteristics most accurately describe your personality? How do you operate on a daily basis?

_____
_____
_____
_____
_____
_____
_____
_____
_____

• What personal values, dreams, and passions do you think about on a regular basis? Why do you want to excel in these areas?

_____
_____
_____
_____
_____
_____
_____
_____
_____

• Based on your answers to these questions, how would you describe your personal mission statement in fifty words or less?

_____
_____
_____
_____

_____
_____
_____
_____
_____
_____

- In light of this mission statement, what top three priorities align with your purposes in life?

_____
_____
_____
_____
_____
_____
_____
_____
_____
_____

- How will you find space for these three priorities on your calendar and ensure that they are given your valuable time?

_____
_____
_____
_____
_____
_____
_____
_____
_____
_____

ESSENTIAL IDEAS TO REMEMBER

Chapter two introduces the keys to unlocking the Maximizer Mindset, which include the following: 1) Find freedom by treasuring truth. 2)

Ignite productivity by prioritizing purpose. 3) Cultivate creativity by leveraging connections.

The Maximizer Mindset empowers individuals in countless personal and professional contexts to work less, achieve more, and spread joy through embracing these three keys. The remainder of the book more deeply delves into providing research, narratives, and real-life applications of these principles.

REFERENCES

Covey, S. R., Merrill, A. R., & Merrill, R. R. (1995). *First things first.* New York: Simon and Schuster.

Covey, S. R. (1989). *The 7 habits of highly effective people: Restoring the character ethic.* New York: Free Press.

Gaille, B. (2021, October 13). *Fifty best personal mission statement examples.* Brandon Gaille Small Business and Marketing Advice. https://brandongaille.com/best-personal-mission-statement/.

Chapter Three

Find Freedom by
Treasuring Truth

"In a time of universal deceit—telling the truth is a revolutionary act."

—George Orwell

In a day in which "fake news" is a common buzzword, fabricated stories are presented as truth, and photoshopped lives are the norm, we find ourselves sorting fact from fiction on a daily basis. And sometimes, it is not that we cannot find the truth . . . It may simply be that we do not want to find it.

DO WE REALLY WANT THE TRUTH?

One of Jack Nicholson's most recognized and repeated cinematic lines is found in *A Few Good Men,* in which he (playing Colonel Nathan R. Jessup) notoriously shouts, "You can't handle the truth!" In his heated testimony addressing Lieutenant Daniel Kaffee (played by Tom Cruise), Colonel Jessup subsequently asserts, "You don't want the truth!" Sometimes, real life plays out in fiction, and for countless individuals, Jessup's words may actually ring true.

Why is it that we sometimes find ourselves neglecting, if not running from, the truth? In *Meditations*, Marcus Aurelius states, "Against our will, our souls are cut off from truth." Along these lines, various psychologists have discovered a number of cognitive biases that alter our views of reality and influence our everyday behaviors and methods of making decisions.

In their book entitled *The Enigma of Reason*, cognitive scientists Hugo Mercier and Dan Sperber (2017) argue that human beings generally possess a common key strength: the ability to justify reconceived beliefs as well as the means of persuading others of these beliefs. This type of reasoning supports us in getting along with others in social contexts, but it also creates a roadblock when it comes to truth-seeking. Additionally, this habit may cause us to fall victim to other cognitive biases, such as confirmation bias, or the propensity to seek out information to support our previously held beliefs.

In spite of the natural desire to avoid the truth, we desperately need to lay hold of the truth in order to decipher what is really happening within our own lives and the lives of others. This is the only means by which we can actually make effective decisions. When we view our world more distinctly through the sharpened lens of the truth, we are better prepared to avoid some of the bumps along the road of life. Along these lines, the truth brings freedom because the blurred viewpoint that corresponds with ignorance limits us.

THE PAINFUL TRUTH OF
COLLECTIVE NARCISSISM

Pain is sometimes associated with learning the truth, but this pain may be exactly what is needed for newfound freedom. One uncomfortable truth becoming increasingly prevalent within today's world is that we as a society seem to be growing ever-more addicted to ourselves. In fact, some might say that the Western world has an issue with narcissism.

A recent study published in *Psychological Science* (Putnam, Ross, Soter, & Roediger, 2019) featured the results of polling slightly fewer than 3,000 Americans across all fifty states. The study discovered that many Americans maintain an oversized and erroneous perception of the role their state has played in U.S. history. Interestingly, there is a term for this phenomenon, namely "collective narcissism."

Lone narcissists hold to a deep-rooted need for validation, and they typically think of themselves as inherently wonderful while resenting anyone else who does not recognize their inherent wonderfulness. By the same token, groups of people who greatly need their group to be recognized as exceptional and admirable may be described as collective narcissists. Lately, the concept of collective narcissism has grown more and more prevalent in psychological contexts, and it is ultimately tied to psychologists' greater concern about a narcissism epidemic, as increasing numbers of individuals maintain exaggerated views of themselves.

At first thought, the likeliest source of blame might be attributed to social media and smartphones that turn average individuals into their own documentarians. Yet, some argue that Instagram, TikTok, Facebook, Twitter, LinkedIn, and the like may not be solely to blame. For example, Will Storr (2018), author of *Selfie: How We Became So Self-Obsessed and What It's Doing to Us*, asserts that Western culture has held these ideals for many years, long before the advent of social media and smartphones. He believes that over time, we have created a cultural norm of exaggerating the part we play in our own victories and failures.

The stories we create within our own minds naturally form our viewpoints regarding truth. Internet culture has steadily heightened our sense of individualism within the Western world. This perception of reality differs significantly from more community-focused, Eastern cultures.

While placing sole emphasis upon individual potential might be tremendously motivating when we receive affirmations such as, "You can accomplish anything you put your mind to!" and "The world is at your fingertips!" such language may ultimately be destructive. This sort of thinking has led to a culture in which we attribute too much credit to ourselves for each and every success, and we place too much blame on ourselves for each and every setback.

In our individualistic society, we often ignore the fact that humans are social beings by nature. We thrive by working together; as John Maxwell famously stated, "Teamwork makes the dream work." Yet, instead of focusing on collaboration, we may find ourselves falling into dangerous mental health traps as we call ourselves "losers" and "failures" when plans fall through. In truth, our victories and setbacks in life result from countless external factors beyond our control. We neglect the truth when we falsely believe that we are solely responsible for all the circumstances of our lives.

Psychologist Richard Nisbett (2013) mapped out the origins of Western individualism in his book *The Geography of Thought: How*

Asians and Westerners Think Differently—and Why. Nisbett traces this predominate sense of individualism to ancient Greece. Consisting of rocky islands with distinct city-states, Greece was a country in which people had to work diligently in individual pursuits in order to achieve success.

For example, rather than taking part in larger farming communities, ancient Greeks found themselves in trades such as foraging or fishing—trades that were inherently more solitary. This prevalent lifestyle eventually cultivated a culture in which selfhood became the ideal, and individuals viewed themselves as the primary means of achievement. This ideal has persisted throughout the history of Western culture into modern thinking.

Nisbett (2013) and his colleagues discovered stark contrasts in the ways Westerners versus Easterners typically operate within society. After conducting studies involving individuals from the West and individuals from the East, they discovered that the thinking processes of people from various regions of the world function as a reflection of their respective cultural histories—histories which were tremendously impacted by geography. For example, the East Asian topography of 2,500 years ago differed significantly from that of Ancient Greece. The people of East Asia found themselves landlocked, with rolling landscapes. In order to achieve success, they created large farming communities, taking part in expansive irrigation endeavors necessary for survival.

As part of his research, Nisbett and colleagues (2013) placed Westerners and Easterners in a lab in which they were asked to observe a cartoon fish tank. This tank held a large, flashy, animated fish along with numerous smaller fish surrounding it. The researchers tracked minute, instinctive eye motion to determine which objects caught people's attention. They found that Western participants seemed more drawn to the larger, flashy fish, while East Asian participants primarily maintained focused on the smaller groups of fish surrounding the larger one.

As the researchers asked that individuals from each group to share what they observed, the Westerners commented that they noticed a fish, whereas the Easterners shared that they observed a fish tank. After the researchers asked each group to share their opinion of the fish, individuals from the West viewed the larger fish as the leader of the group.

Alternatively, those from the East remarked that they felt badly for the larger fish, as it had seemingly been excluded from the group of smaller fish. This study points to the possibility that Western society may entail a more nature focus on self—a focus that is not easily escaped. However, awareness of this focus represents an important first step in breaking away from this mindset.

The third principle of the Maximizer Mindset, "Cultivate creativity by leveraging connections," closely aligns with the first principle, "Find freedom by treasuring truth." The concept of leveraging connections will be expounded upon in chapter five. Nevertheless, in order to fully embrace this principle, we must first face the truth that the cultural phenomenon of collective narcissism prevents even the best intentioned individuals from embracing a Maximizer Mindset. In many cases, rugged individualism ultimately leads to more work, less fulfilling achievements, and less joy, rather than less work, more achievement, and the capacity to spread more joy. By facing the stark fact that narcissism abounds within our culture and being aware of its presence, we also open ourselves to the possibility of going against the grain and living our fullest lives.

BEWARE THE FOUR HORSEMEN

Countless tragic stories of celebrities dying alone as a result of drug overdoses, alcoholism, or taking their own lives points to the harsh reality that even those who seemingly "achieved it all" are susceptible to heartbreaking demises as a result of "looking out for number one." Within the very fabric of our beings, we as humans hunger and thirst for something beyond ourselves. We instinctively long for more.

Even Bertrand Russell (1916), a British philosopher and atheist remarked:

> The center of me is always and eternally a terrible pain—a curious wild pain—a searching for something beyond what the world contains, something transfigured and infinite, the beatific vision—God. I do not find it, I do not think it is to be found, but the love of it is my life . . . it fills every passion I have. It is the actual spring of life in me.

In his book and series *Catholicism: A Journey to the Heart of the Faith,* Father Robert Baron explained:

> Thomas Aquinas said that the four typical substitutes for God are wealth, pleasure, power, and honor. Sensing the void within, we attempt to fill it up with some combination of these four things, but only by emptying out the self in love can we make the space for God to fill us. The classical tradition referred to this errant desire as "concupiscence," but I believe that we could neatly express the same idea with the more contemporary term "addiction." When we try to satisfy the hunger for God with something less than God, we will naturally be frustrated, and then in our frustration, we will convince ourselves that we need more of that finite good, so we will struggle to achieve it, only to find ourselves again, necessarily, dissatisfied. At this point, a sort of spiritual panic sets in, and we can find ourselves turning obsessively around this creaturely good that can never in principle make us happy.

These four substitutes (wealth, pleasure, power, and honor) are often referred to as "the four horsemen," and they intrinsically cultivate an addiction for more within us. Enough is never enough. In fact, modern media is replete with stories of individuals who seemed to have mastered all four of these achievements yet fell to their demise in the midst of money or sex scandals. Every one of us is subject to the temptations of wealth, pleasure, power, and honor.

The life of Solomon, King of Ancient Israel, provides a perfect example of the impact of chasing after the four horsemen to the exclusion of true purpose in life. The Bible offers helpful glimpses into the life of this notable king (I Kings 1–11; II Chronicles 1–9; and 2 Samuel 7, 11–12). Solomon's father was the illustrious King David; his mother, Bathsheeba, was previously married to another man—a soldier David plotted to kill in order to hide their scandalous adultery.

God offered Solomon any one wish he desired, and Solomon asked for wisdom. He became the wisest mortal to walk the earth, mastering countless subjects, and writing 3,000 proverbs, 1,005 songs, and three books of the Bible. He gained unmatched power, and he led as King of Israel for approximately forty years. He supervised the building of a magnificent temple as well as his own splendid palace, devoting seven and thirteen years to these pursuits respectively. His problematic home life included an astounding 700 wives and 300 concubines.

Solomon dedicated his life to answering the pressing question of wide-eyed college students as well as bewildered adults facing mid-life crises—what is the meaning of life? Solomon wholeheartedly hurled himself into all that life might possibly have to offer in pursuit of answering this question. Born into the privileged circumstances of his father David, Solomon sought to indulge his own passions to the fullest. He immersed himself in "living his best life," ultimately realizing that neither wealth, pleasure, power, nor honor could fill a nagging void within him.

Solomon penned Ecclesiastes as a recognition of his own foolishness, a candid autobiography of the superficial life he pursued apart from God. Wearily, Solomon summited his lifetime experiment using a certain word that emerges nearly forty times in the twelve chapters of Ecclesiastes, namely the Hebrew word "hebel." Various Old Testament scholars translate this word in numerous ways, from vanity (ESV, KJV, NASB, NKJV, RSV, NRSV), to emptiness (NEB), to meaningless (NLT, NIV). In other references within the Bible, "hebel" signifies a feathery, transitory, obscure, and swiftly passing vapor. Solomon ultimately pointed to the fact that our fleeting lives are multifaceted; therefore, a multifaceted word most effectively describes life.

Even though the author's viewpoint on life as meaningless seems dismal, his perspective contains great wisdom, keeping in line with his most notable characteristic. The repeated view of life "under the sun" deserves careful reflection. This phrase emerges nearly thirty times throughout Ecclesiastes. Solomon warns the reader not to be deceived into believing that new is improved.

Ecclesiastes is not simply an ancient book; rather, it is an eternal book. It is a timeless work that imparts insights for everyday living. Ecclesiastes was designed to inspire readers to live a life beyond that which takes place "under the sun." Solomon leaves the reader to imagine a reward that exists beyond our vain efforts under the sun, bringing meaning into what so many find to be a meaningless existence. Along those same lines, Charles Spurgeon remarked, "Time is short. Eternity is long. It is only reasonable that this short life be lived in the light of eternity." The life worth living is centered on a cause beyond ourselves, a purpose that will last long after our time on earth is through.

Another astute individual, Albert Einstein, once remarked, "Only a life lived for others is a life worthwhile." What is the truth that sets us free? Maybe this truth involves that fact that life consists of more than our individualistic striving for "more." Solomon and countless others proved that "achieving it all" cannot guarantee a fulfilling existence.

In fact, their lives seem to point to the fact that a reckless abandonment to the pursuit of wealth, pleasure, power, and honor only leads to greater emptiness. The forthcoming chapter discusses the significance of prioritizing purpose. Thinking back to the "Start with why" principle (Sinek, 2011) highlighted in chapter one, life naturally involves a greater sense of purpose and fulfillment as we identify and pursue our "why," beginning with the end in mind.

Each day contains exactly 1,440 minutes. A comparatively small investment of 15 to 30 minutes devoted to deeply, sincerely reflecting upon the questions and challenges below will undoubtedly reap lasting dividends, positively impacting countless areas of life and commencing the journey toward achieving the Maximizer Mindset. Please remember, the following questions are listed for your personal reflection only, and not for anyone else's eyes. The more honestly you answer, the greater your potential for lasting personal growth. The truth ultimately sets us free!

- What evidences of individualism and even narcissism have you seen within your own life? How might you bring others into these areas to support you in cultivating a more collaborative life?

  _____
  _____
  _____
  _____
  _____
  _____
  _____
  _____
  _____
  _____

- How might you rank the four horsemen (wealth, pleasure, power, and honor) in order of importance within your own life? Why does the most important of these pursuits seem so important to you?

_____

_____

_____

_____

_____

_____

_____

_____

_____

_____

_____

- Have you ever found yourself denouncing the four horsemen, only to start chasing them in secret? What steps might you take to replace them with other pursuits (such as the purposes you identified in chapter one)?

_____

_____

_____

_____

_____

_____

_____

_____

_____

- What difficult truths about yourself do you find challenging to address? Why might this be the case?

_____

_____

_____

_____

_____

_____

_____

_____

_____

_____

- What additional steps will you take toward freedom?

_____

_____

_____

_____

_____

_____

_____

_____

_____

ESSENTIAL IDEAS TO REMEMBER

"The truth will set you free" exemplifies a time-tested, yet often over-looked principle. In today's society, it can be challenging to identify the truth, let alone pursue it. At times, we do not feel certain that we can handle the truth, especially the truth about ourselves.

Those who maintain a Maximizer Mindset devote themselves, including their time and active reflection, to deciphering who they are and what motivates them. If these motivations are not in line with their identified purposes in life, they take steps forward in a new direction.

This chapter highlights the significance of "finding freedom by treasuring truth." The remainder of the book builds upon the importance of operating from a place of freedom in the pursuit of the Maximizer Mindset, ultimately creating less work, greater achievement, and more joy.

REFERENCES

Aurelius, M. (2002). *The meditations*. New York: Random House.

Barron, R. E. (2011). *Catholicism: A journey to the heart of the faith*. Image Books.

Mercier, H., & Sperber, D. (2017). *The enigma of reason*. Harvard University Press. https://doi.org/10.4159/9780674977860.

Nisbett, R. (2003). *The geography of thought: How Asians and Westerners think differently—and why*. New York: Free Press.

Putnam, A. L., Ross, M. Q., Soter, L. K., & Roediger, H. L. (2018). Collective narcissism: Americans exaggerate the role of their home state in appraising U.S. history. *Psychological Science, 29*(9), 1414–1422. https://doi.org/10.1177/0956797618772504.

Russell, B. (1967). *The autobiography of Bertrand Russell*. Boston: Little, Brown and Company.

Sinek, S. (2011). *Start with why*. Harlow, England: Penguin Books.

Storr, W. (2018). *Selfie: How we became so self-obsessed and what it's doing to us*. New York: The Overlook Press.

Chapter Four

Ignite Productivity by Prioritizing Purpose

"True happiness . . . is not attained through self-gratification but through fidelity to a worthy purpose."

—Helen Keller

It seems challenging to identify a concept that has garnered more interest in recent years than the principle of the growth mindset. This idea, based on the work of Stanford psychologist Carol Dweck (2016), centers upon the theory that those who believe their abilities can be developed outperform those who believe their abilities are fixed. People who hold to the notion that their talents can be improved over time (through feedback from others, diligent work, and effective strategies) maintain a growth mindset. These individuals often accomplish more than others who hold a fixed mindset (those who maintain the notion that talents are nothing more than innate giftings).

Those who embrace a growth mindset do not waste a great deal of time and energy worrying about whether they appear intelligent. Instead, they invest more time and energy in learning. As entire organizations embrace growth mindset principles, those within the organizations typically begin to feel increasingly empowered and committed to the organization. Additionally, they benefit from heightened opportunities for collaboration and innovation within their work. Contrastingly, individuals within predominately fixed-mindset organizations witness increased deception and cheating among colleagues, ostensibly in pursuit of gains in the race to demonstrate talent.

GROWTH MINDSET MISCONCEPTIONS

Due in large part to findings such as these, the term "growth mindset" has evolved into a common buzzword in countless organizations, sometimes even appearing in their mission statements. Yet, according to Dweck (2016), even those who commonly use the term "growth mindset" may hold a somewhat limited and even erroneous understanding of this idea. In her own words, Dweck (2016) has encountered the following three common misconceptions regarding the growth mindset:

1. I already have it, and I always have. People often confuse a growth mindset with being flexible or open-minded or with having a positive outlook—qualities they believe they've simply always had. My colleagues and I call this a false growth mindset. Everyone is actually a mixture of fixed and growth mindsets, and that mixture continually evolves with experience. A "pure" growth mindset doesn't exist, which we have to acknowledge in order to attain the benefits we seek. (para. 4)

2. A growth mindset is just about praising and rewarding effort. This isn't true for students in schools, and it's not true for employees in organizations. In both settings, outcomes matter. Unproductive effort is never a good thing. It's critical to reward not just effort but learning and progress, and to emphasize the processes that yield these things, such as seeking help from others, trying new strategies, and capitalizing on setbacks to move forward effectively. In all of our research, the outcome—the bottom line—follows from deeply engaging in these processes. (para. 5)

3. Just espouse a growth mindset, and good things will happen. Mission statements are wonderful things. You can't argue with lofty values like growth, empowerment, or innovation. But what do they mean to employees if the company doesn't implement policies that make them real and attainable? They just amount to lip service. Organizations that embody a growth mindset encourage appropriate risk-taking, knowing that some risks won't work out. They reward employees for important and useful lessons learned, even if a project does not meet its original goals. They support collaboration across organizational boundaries rather than competition among employees or units. They are committed to the

growth of every member, not just in words but in deeds, such as broadly available development and advancement opportunities. And they continually reinforce growth mindset values with concrete policies. (para. 6)

Dweck (2016) maintains that the practice of correcting these misconceptions does not necessarily equate to ease in obtaining a growth mindset. Each individual faces unique fixed-mindset triggers. By nature, humans encounter insecurities or defensiveness when faced with challenging setbacks, criticism, or failure. Additionally, organizations that operate as though talent is a fixed concept may ultimately serve to hold stakeholders back from achieving growth-mindset thinking and actions, including collaboration, innovation, opportunities for feedback, and even admitting to mistakes.

Maintaining a growth mindset requires intentional, consistent efforts to identify and work against such triggers. As organizational leaders gain the ability and willingness to recognize fixed-mindset behaviors, they learn to engage in productive self-talk that encourages them to break away from this type of thinking in pursuit of significant goals. Although this is challenging work, organizations and the individuals within them advance greatly by learning more about growth-mindset concepts, ultimately applying them in professional and personal pursuits. This practice provides those involved with a deeper sense of who they truly are and can become, what purposes and principles they stand for, and strategies for moving forward.

THE POTENTIAL FOR GROWING
A GROWTH MINDSET

Countless studies, lectures, and professional development opportunities have centered upon the concept of a growth mindset in recent years. For example, a well-controlled research study involving 6,320 lower-achieving students in secondary schools within the United States focused upon the facilitation of brief online activities designed to support students in developing a growth mindset (Yeager et al., 2019). The researchers discovered that the students who engaged in these online activities eventually saw heightened grades and increasingly enrolled in math courses known to be more challenging.

Another study conducted by researchers from the University of Texas and Stanford University examined the student impact of growth mindset instructional practices and emphasizing a sense of purpose in learning (Paunesku et al., 2015). The researchers explored the impact of these interventions upon student learning experiences, whether these interventions were scalable, and which types of students most greatly benefitted from these interventions.

This study involved 1,594 student participants from thirteen high schools. All participants were placed either within a control group, a group receiving only the growth mindset intervention, a group receiving only a sense of purpose intervention, or a group receiving both a growth mindset intervention coupled with a sense of purpose intervention. All interventions were created to be delivered online in a brief amount of time.

The intervention highlighting growth mindset development entailed one 45-minute online session. This session focused upon the human brain's development, as well as learners' potential to grow in intelligence through practice and study. This session also asked students to summarize their key takeaways through writing a letter to a fellow student.

On the other hand, the intervention highlighting the development of a sense of purpose provided learners with the opportunity to explain the relationship between success at school and achievement of significant goals. Such goals might include "impacting the world in a positive way" or "making my family proud of me."

The researchers ultimately uncovered several key findings:

1. Participants who engaged in intervention involving a growth mindset experienced an increase in their course grades.
2. Participants who identified a sense of purpose experienced an increase in their course grades.
3. Participants who experienced both the growth mindset and sense of purpose interventions were more likely to successfully complete their math, science, and English courses.
4. These findings even more profoundly impacted those participants categorized as academically struggling or at risk.

5. These interventions were discovered to be scalable, appropriate for delivering to larger groups of students in online contexts.

Many studies point to the notion that growth mindset principles, when implemented effectively and consistently, may lead to profound impacts upon performance. On the other hand, it is also apparent that when misinterpreted, this thinking may have a negative impact upon growth and productivity.

PRIORITIZING PURPOSE BEFORE EFFORT

In a day and age in which motivational quotes are endemic on social media and influencers from realms of sports and business tell us that hard work is the sole recipe for success in life, it is easy to overestimate the power of effort. While effort is a necessary ingredient, more is required. Why is it that many people do not find success in spite of how hard they try? The remainder of this chapter focuses upon the value of prioritizing purpose before effort, ultimately unlocking the key to igniting impactful productivity.

While purpose profoundly impacts productivity, purpose and productivity in and of themselves entail two vastly different concepts. Purpose is an often overlooked necessity of a meaningful, healthy existence. Operating in life in accordance with a sense of purpose is not an added bonus or cherry on top. Research supports the fact that purpose represents a vital need for human beings.

According to Alan Rozanski, professor of medicine at the Icahn School of Medicine at Mount Sinai, "Just like people have basic physical needs, like to sleep and eat and drink, they have basic psychological needs . . . The need for meaning and purpose is No. 1 . . . It's the deepest driver of well-being there is" (Gordon, 2019, para. 8–9).

When guided by a clear sense of direction and taking part in endeavors we find personally significant (especially when these endeavors impact someone else), we sense purpose. When life seems ambiguous and we find ourselves mourning distant memories and neglected routines, apathy and discouragement naturally begin to slip into our thinking.

Human beings crave exciting, meaningful reasons to jump out of bed each morning; when these motivating factors do not remain at the forefront of our minds, we begin to feel lost. An overarching purpose in life lifts us out of the temptation toward mental, physical, and emotional slumber. When we operate on the basis of a meaningful sense of purpose, we naturally experience fuller and richer lives and make healthier decisions along the way.

Remaining focused on purpose impacts not only our mental and emotional health, but this mindset also impacts our physical health. Several research studies have discovered a link between longevity and a vibrant sense of purpose. In fact, one study revealed that among middle-aged Americans without an identified sense of purpose, the risk of dying was two times higher throughout a period of four years in comparison to those who maintained a strong sense of purpose (Alimujiang et al., 2019).

The researchers conducting this particular study examined data from almost 7,000 Americans between the ages of 51 and 61 who completed psychological questionnaires regarding the correlation between a sense of purpose in life and morality. The researchers discovered that participants who lacked a strong sense of purpose were prone to die earlier in life; particularly, they faced a greater chance of dying as a result of cardiovascular diseases.

Interestingly, the link between a lacking sense of purpose and earlier death proved true regardless of participants' socioeconomic status, educational experience, race, or gender. Additionally, the researchers discovered this relationship to be so strong that identifying purpose in life appeared more vital for reducing the risk of death than abstaining from smoking or drinking, or even than exercising regularly.

This study contributes to an expanding base of literature regarding the correlation between physical health and purpose in life. Rozanski (2016) utilized data from ten different studies to demonstrate that a solid sense of purpose in life is linked with a lower risk of death and cardiovascular episodes, including strokes and heart attacks.

What matters when it comes to health and longevity, according to researchers (Alimujiang et al., 2019), is not the exact purpose of a person's life, but rather that they have identified a purpose. Whether an individual's purpose involves raising a family, engaging in volunteer work, or impacting others' lives for eternity, a sense of fulfillment will vary from person to person. Purpose in life is something that each individual must carefully and intentionally develop through reflecting upon the answers to essential questions—some of which are listed at the conclusion of this chapter.

Far too many people simply settle for working toward some combination of the following in life: finishing school, obtaining a dream job, finding a romantic relationship, having kids, accumulating professional accolades and promotions, and retiring with a sizeable nest egg. While this list of milestones represents a full life at first glance, the pursuit of checking off a list of objectives is more about life living us. This involves simply following a script, and human beings were created for more in life.

Not only does research demonstrate that a life without purpose leads to poorer health and higher mortality rates, but theology also points to the fact that a lack of purpose in life will lead to emptiness. King Solomon, the final ruler of a united kingdom of Israel, was revered for his wisdom and wealth. As the author of the book of Ecclesiastes in the Bible, Solomon revealed that even the wisest and wealthiest of individuals may ponder the purpose of life while reflecting upon wasted years. Solomon wrote, "Vanity of vanities, says the Preacher, vanity of vanities! All is vanity. What does a man gain by all the toil at which he toils under the sun. A generation goes, and a generation comes, but the earth remains forever" (Ecclesiastes 1:2–4, ESV).

We must reflectively take inventory of our lives and actively consider what we are pouring our efforts toward. This begins with identifying one's purpose in life and actually living this purpose out. Once an individual's purpose has been found, priorities will more naturally fall into place, and productivity will more fully be ignited. It is essential, though, that we focus upon and embrace purpose rather than productivity. Doing so requires an understanding of the differences between the two.

Productivity may be described as the value produced by a task divided by the time required to complete the task. Purpose, on the other hand, is much less quantifiable, although closely correlated with one's health and well-being. Productivity is focused upon outcomes while purpose is focused upon "the why," relating back to the "start with why" principle (Sinek, 2011) discussed in chapter one.

Productivity relates to concrete tasks we accomplish, and these results correlate with our expenditures of time and effort. On the other hand, purpose motivates our commitment to making every moment count and devoting ourselves to a greater cause. If we focus solely or primarily on productivity (as many people do), we will eventually face the threat of waning health, the potential for discouragement, and the danger of burnout.

Focusing on purpose over productivity is the goal, but life also brings countless moments in which productivity is required for survival within our personal and professional contexts. For most people, income follows a tangible output of some kind. Yet, when we face pressures to produce during challenging times, intentionality in keeping purpose at the center of each and every activity supports us in maintaining a balanced life.

Allowing our priorities to flow from purpose helps us to focus and to free ourselves from distractions that are ultimately secondary, tertiary, and beyond. When effort and energy are devoted to priorities aligned with purpose, a much more satisfying life will be the outcome. This leads to the most rewarding type of productivity—the type that energizes and inspires rather than saps strength and leads to frustration.

This second principle of the Maximizer Mindset, "Ignite productivity by prioritizing purpose," closely aligns with the third principle, "Cultivate creativity by leveraging connections." The concept of leveraging connections will be explored more fully in chapter five as a next step in the journey to work less, achieve more, and spread more joy. By placing "people over paper" and "purpose before productivity," we find greater potential to live our lives to the fullest.

Each day contains exactly 1,440 minutes. A comparatively small investment of 15 to 30 minutes devoted to deeply, sincerely reflecting upon the questions and challenges below will undoubtedly reap lasting dividends, positively impacting countless areas of life and commencing the journey toward achieving the Maximizer Mindset. Please remember, the following questions are listed for your personal reflection only, and not for anyone else's eyes. The more honestly you answer, the greater your potential for lasting personal growth. Now is the time to ignite your personal productivity by prioritizing your personal purpose!

- Why does the work you do matter? How is it contributing to bettering the lives of others beyond yourself?

  _____

  _____

  _____

_____
_____
_____
_____
_____
_____
_____

- What are you willing to struggle for?

_____
_____
_____
_____
_____
_____
_____
_____
_____

- If you knew you were going to die one year from now, what would you do? How would you want to be remembered?

_____
_____
_____
_____
_____
_____
_____
_____

- In four sentences or less, how would those around you describe your purpose in life? Feel free to ask a trusted family member or friend if you are unsure!

_____
_____

_____

_____

_____

_____

_____

_____

_____

_____

- How does this align with how you would describe your purpose in life?

_____

_____

_____

_____

_____

_____

_____

_____

- If there is misalignment, what actions (and interactions) might you undertake to help bring about alignment between *your* described purpose and the purpose others observe in your life?

_____

_____

_____

_____

_____

_____

_____

_____

ESSENTIAL IDEAS TO REMEMBER

Ralph Waldo Emerson remarked, "The purpose of life is not to be happy. It is to be useful, to be honorable, to be compassionate, to have it make some difference that you have lived and lived well." Those who maintain a Maximizer Mindset devote time, energy, effort, and careful thought to determining who they are and what inspires them. They set priorities that directly align with their purposes in order to propel productivity for mission-critical pursuits.

This chapter highlights the significance of "igniting productivity by prioritizing purpose." The following chapters of the book build upon the essential foundation of operating from a position of purposeful living in the pursuit of the Maximizer Mindset, ultimately creating less work, greater achievement, and more joy.

REFERENCES

Alimujiang, A., Wiensch, A., Boss, J., Fleischer, N. L., Mondul, A. M., McLean, K., . . . & Pearce, C. L. (2019). Association between life purpose and mortality among US adults older than 50 years. *JAMA Network Open, 2*(5), e194270-e194270.

Cohen, R., Bavishi, C., & Rozanski, A. (2016). Purpose in life and its relationship to all-cause mortality and cardiovascular events: A meta-analysis. *Psychosomatic Medicine, 78*(2), 122–33.

Dweck, C. (2016). What having a "growth mindset" actually means. *Harvard Business Review, 13*, 213–26.

Gordon, M. (2019, May 25). *What's your purpose? Finding a sense of meaning in life is linked to health.* NPR. https://www.npr.org/sections/health-shots/2019/05/25/726695968/whats-your-purpose-finding-a-sense-of-meaning-in-life-is-linked-to-health.

Paunesku, D., Walton, G. M., Romero, C., Smith, E. N., Yeager, D. S., & Dweck, C. S. (2015). Mind-set interventions are a scalable treatment for academic underachievement. *Psychological Science, 26*(6), 784–93.

Sinek, S. (2011). *Start with why.* Harlow, England: Penguin Books.

Xerri, M. J., Radford, K., & Shacklock, K. (2018). Student engagement in academic activities: A social support perspective. *Higher Education, 75*, 589–605. https://doi.org/10.1007/s10734-017-0162-9.

Yeager, D. S., Hanselman, P., Walton, G. M. et al. (2019). A national experiment reveals where a growth mindset improves achievement. *Nature, 573*, 364–69. https://doi.org/10.1038/s41586-019-1466-y.

Chapter Five

Cultivate Creativity by Leveraging Connections

"I am convinced that material things can contribute a lot to making one's life pleasant, but, basically, if you do not have very good friends and relatives who matter to you, life will be really empty and sad and material things cease to be important."

—David Rockefeller

In a world in which individualism is often prized, far too many overlook the power of connectivity. In fact, creativity flourishes through effective collaboration, but not all partnerships are created equal. This chapter presents practical steps for discovering, developing, and capitalizing upon "perfect pairings" to cultivate creativity.

Our lives ought to be measured by the quality and depth of our relationships. If loving others is our priority, everything else will fall in line. Knock down this kingpin, and the rest will follow. If we prioritize everything else first but don't get this right, our lives will not ultimately be fulfilling, period. If there's one thing to "maximize," it is our relationships! This is our deepest human need.

Microwave-style, instant relationships will never work out very well. The most genuine, lasting relationships require intentionally devoted time and effort. When we invest in relationships and put other human beings first—without focusing on what we will receive in return—we will ultimately receive more than we could ever imagine. This type of thinking—and living—requires work on our parts, as it is easier to be selfish and self-centered. This is especially true in today's individualistic world.

THE INEVITABILITY OF INCREASING
INDIVIDUALISM

While individualism is believed to be increasing among Western cultures, research also suggests that the perception of individualism may be rising around the world. In fact, heightened socioeconomic expansion is a particularly powerful predictor of more common individualistic behaviors and values within a country over time (Santos, Varnum, & Grossmann, 2017).

According to Henri Santos of the University of Waterloo, "Much of the research on the manifestation of rising individualism—showing, for example, increasing narcissism and higher divorce rates—has focused on the United States. Our findings show that this pattern also applies to other countries that are not Western or industrialized . . . Although there are still cross-national differences in individualism-collectivism, the data indicate that, overall, most countries are moving towards greater individualism" (Santos & Grossmann, 2017, para. 2).

Generally, individualist societies view people as self-sufficient, and they often view autonomy and individuality as values associated with their culture. Alternatively, collectivist cultures commonly see people as linked with fellow human beings within a broader social framework. They often highlight interdependency, familial connections, and conformity to social norms (Santos & Grossmann, 2017).

To investigate individualistic behaviors across various cultures, Santos and Grossman (2017) explored data such as the size of households, rates of divorce, and the segment of single-person households. In order to quantify individualistic mindsets, they analyzed statistics regarding the value people place on friends in comparison to family, the significance parents place on teaching children how to be independent, and people's emphasis upon self-expression as a goal (Santos & Grossmann, 2017).

In an effort to identify changes in individualistic behaviors over time, the researchers examined explicit socio-ecological influences such as socioeconomic growth, disaster incidence, and frequency of communicable disease. Generally, the findings demonstrated a definite pattern in the rise of individualistic habits and values around the world (Santos & Grossmann, 2017).

Several socio-ecological factors—including more frequent disasters, less prevalent infectious disease, and less climatic stress in poorer countries—were linked with individualism, but increased socioeconomic development was the strongest predictor of increased individualism over time. Various aspects of development were related to increases in individualism, particularly increases in the percentage of white-collar employment, in educational attainment, and in household incomes (Santos & Grossmann, 2017).

As more and more cultures idolize productivity, the value of relationships is increasingly becoming a secondary, tertiary, or even lesser consideration. In a world in which "looking out for number one" is often encouraged—even if at times not overtly—other people's needs may be considered nothing more than an inconvenience. When production is placed before people and individualism is idolized, we face the danger of missing out on "the stuff of life."

THE VITALITY OF RELATIONAL INVESTMENT

Although we may logically recognize that relationships matter when it comes to happiness in life, we may not realize how significantly relationships impact our health. How do connections with others benefit us, and how does a lack of connection harm us? Solid relationships comprise an essential component of a healthy life, according to research that demonstrates that strong connections with others elongate our lives, enable us to more effectively handle stress, and encourage us to develop healthier daily habits.

Researchers have discovered that individuals in solid, long-term relationships are half as likely to die prematurely than those without such relationships. An existence without relationships is actually as unhealthy as smoking when it comes to life expectancy (Holt-Lunstad, Smith, & Layton, 2010). As social beings, our relationships impact our health mentally, emotionally, and physically.

The quality of the relationships we maintain is the greatest predictor of our quality of life—greater than financial success, wealth, fame, or status. Another study, the Harvard Study of Adult Development (https://www.adultdevelopmentstudy.org/), among the longest-running research studies to examine the life span of adult males, found that the quality of human connectedness aligns with both heightened happiness and greater longevity. This points to the fact that relationships affect our emotional as well as physical well-being. Human beings were created to live in community; we most naturally thrive from a mental, emotional, and physical perspective when pursuing, developing, and cultivating quality relationships with others.

THE POWER OF PRIORITIZING PEOPLE

Tennessee Williams remarked, "Life is partly what we make it, and partly what it is made by the friends we choose." Our intentional investment in the lives of those around us can make for an incredible life. The power of prioritizing people creates ripple effects in every area of life, including both personal and professional spheres. Yet, this can be difficult to do when each and every day of our lives is jam-packed with various "to-dos." Strategies exist for putting people over productivity while still successfully accomplishing the tasks that must be done.

Our schedules must have margin in order for quality relationships to develop and thrive. In general, meaningful connections are not scheduled and do not take place in accordance with an agenda. They transpire as a result of us making ourselves available to others and demonstrating an interest in who they are as people—even apart from their professional identities. When we find our calendars tightly packed with plan after plan, we will likely find ourselves unable to engage in priority management, mentioned in the previous chapter, which includes the priority of purposeful interactions with people. We will inevitably find ourselves dropping the ball time after time, leaving little time for the important work of building relationships.

This principle aligns with the strategy of under-promising and over-delivering. When we intentionally leave a bit of leeway in our daily schedules, we better position ourselves to actually accomplish the priorities that need to be accomplished. This practice also leaves space for building relationships with those around us, apart from an inflexible agenda.

A bit of margin in our schedules allows for time to check in with those around us, which is a vital component of relational investment. This might be as simple as dropping by a colleague's desk to ask about what they are excited to be working on, calling a family member to allow them to share the highs and lows of their past week, or scheduling a meeting with a friend who has been experiencing a difficult season. If this seems to be a daunting task, it may simply be that this is a somewhat atypical practice that will take time to develop. It is perfectly fine to take baby steps, intentionally building in moments for investment in key relationships.

In our digital age of all-encompassing smart phones, all-consuming social media, ever-present text messages, and consistently overflowing email inboxes, virtual relationships that require less genuine investment often serve to mask the importance of honest, deep relationships. There is temptation to avoid potential heartache and pain that may occur if time, effort, and energy are invested without reciprocation.

Many people fill their schedules with professional pursuits, entertainment, or any other distractions available to avoid genuine relationships with others. The fact remains that as we strive to protect ourselves from relationships that do not fall into place as expected, we wander ever farther from the intended purpose of our lives. Relational investment may not always be easy or convenient, but a full, meaningful life cannot be lived without it. In his classic book *The Four Loves*, C. S. Lewis (1960) shared the following truths regarding the dangers of life without community:

> To love at all is to be vulnerable. Love anything, and your heart will certainly be wrung and possibly be broken. If you want to make sure of keeping it intact, you must give your heart to no one, not even to an animal. Wrap it carefully round with hobbies and little luxuries; avoid all entanglements; lock it up safe in the casket or coffin of your selfishness. But in that casket—safe, dark, motionless, airless—it will change. It will not be broken; it will become unbreakable, impenetrable, irredeemable. The alternative to tragedy, or at least to the risk of tragedy, is damnation. The only place outside Heaven where you can be perfectly safe from all the dangers and perturbations of love is Hell. (pp. 169–70)

Getting our priorities right also helps us focus and get rid of distractions that are ultimately secondary, tertiary, and beyond. By directing our energy and effort toward people first, we will have a much more satisfying life. This not only includes our families, friends, and neighbors but also colleagues. In fact, many of us spend most of our waking hours

alongside coworkers. This brings a great deal of time to either build colleagues up with words of encouragement, or to remain silent. It is vital
that we actively reflect upon what sorts of memories, if any, we hope
to leave with those we spend more time alongside than nearly anyone
else in life. Not only is it possible to prioritize people while still accomplishing the tasks that must be done, but placing others first also allows
us to more meaningfully and effectively complete the necessary tasks.

WINNING FRIENDS AND INFLUENCING PEOPLE

As a former salesman, author Dale Carnegie's success in sales led to his
territory becoming the national leader for his firm. Carnegie eventually
moved from sales to teaching public speaking, allowing him to earn
$500 per week—equal today to $11,800. Even Warren Buffet partici-
pated in Carnegie's course when he was twenty years old.

Carnegie deeply valued the power of prioritizing people. His principles were encapsulated in the classic book *How to Win Friends and
Influence People* (1964).

Below are several principles for navigating relationships to live by:

Don't criticize, condemn, or complain.

Psychologist B. F. Skinner conducted research studies demonstrating that when animals are rewarded for positive behaviors, they learn
more quickly and retain more effectively than when they are punished
for negative behaviors. Since Skinner's studies were conducted, fur-
ther research has demonstrated that this concept pertains to humans
also . . . Criticizing will not yield positive results. Lasting change
will never come from criticism; in fact, criticism often only results in
resentment. People are creatures of emotion, not logic, who are often
motivated by ego and pride.

Give honest and sincere appreciation.

Most wants in people's lives (for example, the desire for food, sleep,
money) are usually or eventually gratified; however, one longing—
almost as deeply embedded as the longing for sleep or food—is not as

frequently met: the desire to be seen as important. By default, we too often take those in our lives for granted. Through heartfelt, intentional words of affirmation, we hold the potential to transform other's views of themselves, heighten their motivation, and propel their success. When considering the fact that offering genuine appreciation costs us nothing and can so greatly improve another person's life, what could possibly stop us from offering encouragement to others?

Arouse in other people an eager want.

Lloyd George, the prime minister of Great Britain throughout World War I who remained in power for years after other wartime leaders, was once asked to share strategies for remaining on top over the years. His response was simple yet profound . . . He discovered how important it is to "bait the hook to suit the fish." Simply stated, it is imperative to offer people what they value and desire rather than what you value and desire. This principle vastly impacts our ability to impact others. We must frame opportunities in terms that motivate them. This is not possible until we are able to view situations from other people's viewpoints rather than only from our own personal perspective.

Far too many people spend their lifetimes without viewing situations from other people's perspectives. When we place our own thoughts, perspectives, and desires aside and shift our viewpoint to other people's perspectives, we will be more effective in persuading people to partner with us in accomplishing important goals. Those who attempt to unselfishly serve others hold a tremendous advantage over so many who spend their lives looking out for themselves. As Carnegie famously stated, "You can make more friends in two months by becoming interested in other people than you can in two years by trying to get other people interested in you."

POWERFUL PAIRINGS

Much like some of the greatest duos in history—whether real or fictional—human beings can exist without one another, but we absolutely should not. These duos represent powerful pairings whose summative value is staggering. Many elements of life are simply better together.

For example, a person could eat a slice of cheese (and it will be delicious) and separately enjoy a slice of ham (and it will be tasty), but by placing them together in one sandwich, the best is yet to come.

Powerful pairings provide consistent examples of the fact, as Aristotle stated, that "the whole is greater than the sum of its parts." Some of the greatest duos in history might be compared to popcorn and the movies, macaroni and cheese, or peanut butter and jelly . . . They are simply better together. Furthermore, some of these duos are unexpected and unlikely pairs.

For example, consider Batman and Alfred. The dynamic duo of Batman and Robin likely first comes to mind. As we think about this more deeply, though, without Robin, Batman would not have a crime-fighting partner. Without Alfred, Batman would not be alive. Alfred served as an essential component of Batman's crime-fighting endeavors; his partnership made all the difference. Other essential partnerships include Adam and Eve, Tom Brady and Rob Gronkowski, Wanda and Vision, and Anna and Elsa.

Those who believe they will be able to (or already have) accomplished greatness alone are delusional; there is no such thing as a self-made person! These relationships are built upon shared trust (even through complex and challenging trials), common values and goals, and complimentary and distinctive skills. These powerful pairings will never occur unless we prioritize relationships. We must also realize that in many situations, unplanned experiences occur as a result of thoughtful collaboration. As we say "yes" to both planned and unplanned opportunities together, the sky is the limit, and the greatest adventures unfold.

Each day contains exactly 1,440 minutes. A comparatively small investment of 15 to 30 minutes devoted to deeply, sincerely reflecting upon the questions and challenges below will undoubtedly reap lasting dividends, positively impacting countless areas of life and commencing the journey toward achieving the Maximizer Mindset. Please remember, the following questions are listed for your personal reflection only, and not for anyone else's eyes. The more honestly you answer, the greater your potential for lasting personal growth. Now is the time to cultivate creativity by leveraging connections!

- On a scale from 1 to 10, with 10 being the highest rating, take a moment to rate how satisfied you are with your relationships. How satisfied are you with this number?

  _____
  _____
  _____
  _____
  _____
  _____
  _____
  _____
  _____
  _____

- Do you wish this number was higher? If so, think of three relationships you would like to be stronger. List them below . . .

  _____
  _____
  _____
  _____
  _____
  _____
  _____
  _____
  _____

- For each of the relationships you listed above, reflect on one next step you can take to intentionally invest in each one. Write them below, including a timeline for fulfilling each of these next steps . . .

  _____
  _____
  _____
  _____
  _____
  _____
  _____

_____
_____
_____

ESSENTIAL IDEAS TO REMEMBER

As author Mandy Hale remarked, "'Too busy is a myth.' People make time for the things that are really important to them." In our mile-a-minute world, when life seems full of tasks to accomplish, there has never been a time in which intentionalism in relationship building is more vital. Relationships do not only support us in thriving, but they represent an essential component of our survival. Those who develop a Maximizer Mindset give their time, energy, and effort to investing in the lives of others.

This chapter highlights the importance of "cultivating creativity by leveraging connections." The following chapters of the book build upon the key foundations of operating from a standpoint of purpose-filled living in the quest to develop the Maximizer Mindset, ultimately fostering a life of less work, greater achievement, and more joy.

REFERENCES

Boullier, M., & Blair, M. (2018). Adverse childhood experiences. *Pediatrics and Child Health, 28*(3), 132–37.

Carnegie, D. (1964). *How to win friends and influence people.* New York: Simon and Schuster.

Lewis, C. S. (1960). *The four loves.* New York: Harcourt, Brace, Jovanovich.

Holt-Lunstad, J., Smith, T. B., & Layton, J. B. (2010). Social relationships and mortality risk: A meta-analytic review. *PLoS Medicine, 7*(7), e1000316. https://doi.org/10.1371/journal.pmed.1000316.

Santos, H. C., & Grossmann, I. (2017). *Individualistic practices and values increasing around the world.* Association for Psychological Sciences. https://www.psychologicalscience.org/news/releases/individualistic-practices-and-values-increasing-around-the-world.html.

Santos, H. C., Varnum, M. E. W., & Grossmann, I. (2017). Global increases in individualism. *Psychological Science, 28*(9), 1228–39. https://doi.org/10.1177/0956797617700622.

Chapter Six

Adding Value through the Maximizer Mindset

"Dig deep enough in every heart and you'll find it: a longing for meaning, a quest for purpose. As surely as a child breathes, he will someday wonder, What is the purpose of my life?"

—Max Lucado

The Maximizer Mindset encourages and empowers individuals to add value to their lives and the lives of others. Those who embrace this mindset achieve freedom by seeking truth, spark productivity by prioritizing purpose, and promote creativity by leveraging connections. In doing so, they bring infinite value to various contexts of life, including family and social dynamics, professional spheres, and areas of service.

Additionally, they naturally inspire others in obtaining newfound freedom, gaining remarkable productivity, and unlocking powerful creativity as they work toward their own goals in life. This chapter focuses upon the inherent, priceless result of unlocking the Maximizer Mindset, namely adding value to all areas of life—primarily through focusing upon adding value to the lives of others.

TAKERS, GIVERS, AND MATCHERS

Everyone spends some of their time throughout each day as a "taker" and some of their time throughout each day as a "giver." This variance between the two is a natural part of existing and functioning on earth alongside other human beings. Yet, for each of us, the scales may tip at any given time (or even during most times) toward either a propensity for taking or a propensity for giving. We may altruistically hope that the scales lean more often in the direction of giving, and yet for most of us, our basic human instincts point toward taking (even while possibly believing ourselves to be giving).

As a quick assessment of the propensity for either taking or giving, spend several moments pondering the following scenario:

Pretend that you are meeting a friend for dinner, and this friend mentions that they are in the process of looking for a new career opportunity. They share that they are interested in working within an organization in which you personally know a hiring manager. However, it has been a number of years since you spoke to this manager. What would your course of action (or inaction) be?

1. You enthusiastically offer to make an introduction in order to support your friends' professional aspirations.
2. You offer to make an introduction. Later along in the conversation, you request your friend's help with a professional issue you are currently facing.
3. You don't mention that you know the hiring manager at this company. It seems somewhat inconvenient and possibly even uncomfortable to reach out to the hiring manager, considering you haven't spoken in several years.

Our natural reactions to scenarios such as this reflect our "reciprocity style," which, according to Adam Grant (2013), author of *Give and Take: A Revolutionary Approach to Success*, categorizes the way in which we handle interactions with those around us. In his book, Grant offers three reciprocity styles, namely takers, givers, and matchers.

As the name implies, takers demonstrate self-focused behaviors, placing their personal interests before the needs of others. They naturally attempt to benefit as greatly as possible from each interaction while simultaneously giving as little as possible in return.

Matchers, on the other hand, seek to maintain an equal balance between taking and giving. Their natural mindset leans toward thoughts such as: "I take from those who take from me; I give to those who give to me."

Finally, givers focus upon others and lean toward giving to others without strings attached. They ponder such questions as, "What can I do to add value to the lives of those within my spheres of influence? What can I contribute to make someone else's life better?"

As each of us reflect upon which category we most often fall within, most individuals land someplace in the middle, in the matcher category. Human beings innately function in a reciprocal manner; givers and takers signify extremes along the spectrum. Givers represent the more generous individuals among us, but matchers also play a significant part in our society. For example, they more often demonstrate a propensity for ensuring that "what goes around, comes around." They naturally award givers for their kind actions; they also more instinctively seek out revenge in the face of mistreatment of others.

Interestingly enough, givers often comprise the worst performers in workplace situations, according to Grant's (2013) studies. Within a number of professional contexts, givers find themselves at a disadvantage when they sacrifice their personal success in order to help others succeed. Yet, this does not imply that the highest performers fall within the matchers or takers category. In fact, once again, givers find themselves amongst the top performers within professional settings. Surprisingly, the lowest and highest performers fall within the givers category, with takers and matchers someplace in between.

This unexpected phenomenon makes sense when considering the fact that takers naturally acquire reputations as those who place themselves before others, while matchers naturally seek to reciprocate, possibly finding ways in which to knock takers down a peg or two. For this reason, takers typically fail in the areas of creating substantial relationships and collegial networks. Alternatively, matchers characteristically cheer givers on toward success, naturally seeking to match one positive action for another.

Those who work alongside givers trust and support them, as they can be depended upon to consistently add value to other's lives and to enhance the success of those within their circles. Ultimately, givers find great success as a result of the genuine relationships they cultivate, which bring benefit to their lives as well as to the lives of others. As they build solid relationships, they naturally experience greater joy in life than others who simply take, take, take.

One may wonder, though, why some givers operate at the lower levels of professional performance, especially considering givers' propensity toward relational development and greater joy. According to Grant (2013), two types of givers exist in this world, namely "otherish" givers and "selfless" givers.

As the name suggests, selfless givers make a practice of dropping anything and everything to provide assistance for anyone and everyone, all the time. As a result of this tendency, they often fall behind on the tasks that must be accomplished. This may naturally cause them to reside among the poorer performers in professional settings; yet, they are still typically richer in joy than takers.

Alternatively, otherish givers most often give in insightful and strategic ways, as they have developed the ability to proactively navigate relationships with both takers and matchers, making it less likely that those around them will take advantage of their willingness to give of themselves for the sake of others.

THE TRAITS OF SUCCESSFUL GIVERS

For those who find themselves earnestly desiring to be successful givers, a number of steps can be taken to achieve this way of living—a way of living which results in healthier relationships, greater joy, and higher achievement at work.

1. Five-minute favors: Help others with small favors that can be accomplished in five minutes or less, such as offering applicable advice, facilitating an introduction, or providing feedback. Accomplishing these brief yet impactful favors for others can truly make a positive impact toward strengthening relationships.
2. Ask for help: Seek out a colleague's or friend's support regarding an issue you are experiencing while not requesting a great deal of their time. Although this initially involves asking for something rather than giving something, it provides someone else with the opportunity to be a giver, allowing them to feel insightful and to experience the joy of being helpful. According to Grant (2013), one of the most significant methods for cultivating solid relationships is through seeking advice, as it provides the opportunity

to contribute to another's life and to experience fulfillment in this pursuit.

3. Specialize in acts of service: Select certain ways of supporting others at which you truly excel, and then leverage these gifts to the benefits of others. This will cause your service to others to feel energizing rather than exhausting; this saves the potential for burnout through attempting to be a jack of all trades. This will also support you in gaining a reputation for areas of expertise you are willing to share instead of as someone who is available for any and every need at all times.

Ultimately, the essence of becoming a successful giver involves becoming an authentic giver. By avoiding the temptation to give in order to get, we will be well on our way to adding value to the lives of others through meaningful giving endeavors.

Below are additional questions taken from Grant's (2013) *Give and Take* assessment to help in the quest to determine whether we are takers, givers, or matchers:

1. You and a stranger will both receive some money. You have three choices about what you and the stranger receive, and you'll never see or meet the stranger. Which option would you choose?
   a. I get $8, and the stranger gets $4.
   b. I get $5, and the stranger gets $7.
   c. I get $5, and the stranger gets $5.

2. In 2006, after the devastation caused by Hurricane Katrina, a US bank executive led a team of employees on a trip to help rebuild New Orleans. Why do you think he did this?
   a. He wanted to make headlines for being a generous, giving organization.
   b. He felt compassion for the victims and wanted to do whatever he could to help.
   c. He wanted to show his support for bank employees who had family members in New Orleans.

3. You're applying for a job as a manager, and a former boss writes you a glowing recommendation letter. What would you be most likely to do?

a. Go out of my way to make a good impression on my new boss, so I can line up another strong recommendation for the future.
b. Offer to write a recommendation letter for one of my own former employees, so I can pay it forward.
c. Look for ways to help my former boss, so I can pay it back.

4. You're working on a project with two colleagues, and there are three tasks that need to get done. As you discuss how to divide tasks, it becomes clear that all three of you are extremely interested in two of the tasks but view the third as quite boring. What would you do?
a. Try to convince one of my colleagues to do the boring task.
b. Volunteer for the boring task without asking for anything in return.
c. Volunteer for the boring task and ask my colleagues for a favor later.

5. A few years ago, you helped an acquaintance named Jamie find a job. You've been out of touch since then. All of a sudden, Jamie sends an email introducing you to a potential business partner. What's the most likely motivation behind Jamie's email?
a. Jamie wants to ask for help again.
b. Jamie genuinely wants to help me.
c. Jamie wants to pay me back.

According to Grant (2013), those who select mostly A's are takers, mostly B's are givers, and mostly C's are matchers. As we reflect upon scenarios such as those listed above, we may realize that although we sometimes (or even often) lean toward propensities demonstrated by takers, we greatly desire to be givers. In order words, even though we naturally gravitate toward ourselves, we would like to more intentionally focus upon others. The willingness and desire to focus on others is key to adding value to the lives of those around us, which is at the heart of the Maximizer Mindset.

ADDING VALUE IN EVERY INTERACTION

How might our lives—and the lives of those around us—be different if we adopted the mindset that *literally* every single interaction—both great and small—represents a fresh opportunity to add value to someone else's life? For example, how might our trips to the grocery store, the post office, the coffee shop, and so on, be altered if we approached each of these situations with a concern for those around us?

How might our dealings with the next cashier, postal worker, or barista be impacted if we approached these moments with the desire to add value to the lives of those we interact with, moment by moment? What if these experiences, instead of being handled with a "Let's get this done!" mindset were approached with a "How can I add value?" mindset? What if we viewed ourselves as holding the potential to make each day a little brighter for those around us through our words and actions? Is it possible that even the most seemingly mundane situations could be infused with more meaning—and even more joy?

Practically, we accomplish this goal by starting small with an ordinary task, such as visiting the grocery store. An everyday conversation can be completely transformed through taking three actions that most people never think to do:

1. Look others in the eyes.
2. Smile at them.
3. Ask questions.

Jerry Wiles (2020), president emeritus of Living Water International, explains:

Connecting with people and making new friends is not as difficult as we might think. Sometimes all it takes is a smile, a friendly greeting, a comment, or a question. Being alert and watching for those opportunities can make a difference in whether we connect with what God is doing in people's lives, or missing those opportunities. It's easy to be so focused on our shopping lists that we fail to notice the people around us. On a recent shopping trip, I simply asked a lady who was looking over the meat selections, "Are you a salmon connoisseur?" Well, that question opened a conversation, and she began telling me about her shopping practices. I complimented a store worker and expressed my appreciations for the way they arranged their products in the store. That lead to a conversation about the worker's recent move from Detroit to Houston. (para.1–2)

How might our professional experiences be altered if we approached our jobs in this way? How might our mindset toward "the daily grind" be impacted if instead of viewing our work as a "grind," we viewed it as a professional calling through which to add value to the lives of others? Rather than simply considering our work as an opportunity to earn a paycheck, what if we viewed it as an opportunity to meaningfully connect with and bring joy to others? What would happen if we did this—and this is tricky—without the expectation of reciprocity?

THE GOLDEN RULE

Each day, countless parents and teachers around the world advise children to abide by some form of the "Golden Rule"; from a very young age, most of us receive encouragement to treat others as we would like to be treated. This concept is not new to us, and yet it is often frequently misunderstood. In today's "dog eat dog" society, the Golden Rule may instead be interpreted as, "He who has the gold makes the rules." This may be true in some contexts, but it ultimately misses the point. Those who understand the Maximizer Mindset understand why this is not the ideal.

In Jesus Christ's Sermon on the Mount, He declares, "Do unto others as you would have them do unto you." He utilizes this statement as a means of summarizing the Law and the Prophets. Although some regard His declaration as a simple statement that directs us toward the goal of being nice, few actually realize that the Golden Rule is the foundation of all free market economies, entrepreneurship, and of modern civilization as a whole (Martin, 2015).

Anyone who wants to make money, such as a salesperson or businessperson in nearly any industry, will need to be able to solve other people's issues in order to generate revenue. Although for some, the word "salesman" brings to mind a fast-talking, plaid-jacket-wearing trickster eagerly pouncing upon unsuspecting customers at a used car lot, this sort of thinking is often founded upon a false belief about salespeople.

Many assume that there exists only a limited amout of wealth in the world; along those lines, they presume that one may gain only when another loses. They view life as a zero-sum game. If we ponder many of the greatest gains and losses in human history, including various wars and imperial conquests, we realize that much of humanity believes that in order to gain anything for oneself, something else must be lost by someone else.

What we fail to realize is that wealth is not limited to buried treasure in the sand or billions of dollars stashed away in a miser's vault. Rather, wealth "can be created in unlimited qualities, limited only by man's creativity and the constraints under which he works" (Martin, 2015, para. 11). If we think of the case of the salesman, he ultimately holds no claim to other's money; instead, he must influence someone else to buy from him.

Although his ability to persuade others is often seen in a negative light, perhaps as a seductive power of some sort, how many of us have actually been "seduced" to purchase a car? Rather, most people need a means of transportation from place to place; they ultimately buy a car out of need rather than seduction. Maybe the salesman who closes the deal is more skilled at selling than the customer is at buying, but this cannot be blamed on the salesman. Yes, he is capable of cheating customers—and yes, some salesmen do. Either the courts or their reputations eventually catch up with cheaters.

Most salespeople—as with most entrepreneurs in general—simply operate from the perspective of seeking to support themselves and their families. And, in the case of the car salesman, he needs income—more than the cars he sells. And the customer needs a car—more than the money they have available to spend. Making the exchange of a car for the money it costs leads to both the customer and the salesman becoming richer.

As we multiply this principle across our entire society, it becomes clear that countless jobs exist because of inventions such as automobiles and exchanges such as this. The compound effect over time is astounding, and the ability for entrepreneurs to pursue their creative visions has brought us into the modern world. As new products and services are designed and sold, they solve problems.

As we think back to the Golden Rule and how this applies to the salesman, he makes sales as a result of his ability to persuade—but he must first solve another person's problem. This is the key to it all (Martin, 2015). Success in sales, much like success in life, involves the ability to place ourselves in another person's shoes, understanding their situation, their preferences, their issues, and their needs.

Salesmen, entrepreneurs, leaders, teachers, and professionals of every kind find success through solving the problems of others. The Golden Rule truly is the secret to success; people not only make a living though solving other people's issues, but they also achieve greater good, ultimately impacting their communities—and possibly even the world—for the better. Focusing upon treating others as we want to be treated, thus imparting value to other's lives—will also add value to our own lives.

Each day contains exactly 1,440 minutes. A comparatively small investment of 15 to 30 minutes devoted to deeply, sincerely reflecting upon the questions and challenges below will undoubtedly reap lasting dividends, positively impacting countless areas of life and commencing the journey toward achieving the Maximizer Mindset. Please remember, the following questions are listed for your personal reflection only, and not for anyone else's eyes. The more honestly you answer, the greater your potential for lasting personal growth. Now is the time to add value to the lives of others through the Maximizer Mindset, thus adding value to your own life as a result!

- Reflecting back upon the quiz you took previously in this chapter, do you seem to be more of a taker, a giver, or a matcher? How satisfied are you with this conclusion?

_____
_____
_____
_____
_____
_____
_____
_____
_____
_____

- Do you wish this conclusion was different? If so, what motivations and thought patterns need to be altered?

_____

_____

_____

_____

_____

_____

_____

_____

_____

- What steps will you take now in order to begin making these changes?

_____

_____

_____

_____

_____

_____

_____

_____

_____

- Who will you enlist to support you in this journey?

_____

_____

_____

_____

_____

_____

_____

_____

_____

- What is an example in which someone used their innovative mindset to help you solve a problem you were facing?

  _____
  _____
  _____
  _____
  _____
  _____
  _____
  _____
  _____
  _____

- How might you also do this for someone else in the coming days?

  _____
  _____
  _____
  _____
  _____
  _____
  _____
  _____
  _____
  _____

ESSENTIAL IDEAS TO REMEMBER

As Rosa Parks wisely remarked, "Nothing in the Golden Rule says that others will treat us as we have treated them. It only says that we must treat others in a way that we would want to be treated." Although we cannot predict or control the actions of others, those who maintain a Maximizer Mindset navigate their treatment of others to reflect the ways they want to be treated, consistently seeking to add value to others' lives. They endeavor to be givers because they treasure the opportunity to play some part in solving problems that others face, using their creativity to meet specific needs.

This chapter highlights the importance of "adding value through the Maximizer Mindset." The final chapter of the book reflects essential ideas to remember and apply in the quest to develop the Maximizer Mindset, ultimately nurturing a life of less work, greater achievement, and more joy.

REFERENCES

Grant, A. M. (2013). *Give and take: A revolutionary approach to success.* New York: Viking.

Martin, R. D. (2015, August 26). *What's the secret to success? Abide by the Golden Rule.* Inc. https://www.inc.com/quora/what-s-the-secret-to-success-abide-by-the-golden-rule.html.

Wiles, J. (2020, January 2). *The alertness factor: Connecting with God's redemptive activity.* Assist News Service. https://www.assistnews.net/the-alertness-factor-connecting-with-gods-redemptive-activity/.

Chapter Seven

Essential Ideas to Remember

"Don't be fooled by the calendar. There are only as many days in the year as you make use of. One man gets only a week's value out of a year while another man gets a full year's value out of a week."

—Charles Richards

As we reflect upon the various facets of the Maximizer Mindset, our "why" would not be complete without exploring how we might apply this mindset to various aspects of everyday life. The Maximizer Mindset provides space to focus on winning in the areas of life that truly matter.

Individuals who embrace this mindset understand that giving it your all, all the time, is not what counts. In fact, this will likely result in frustration, burnout, failure, and alienation. Those who take on the Maximizer Mindset instead focus on substance before style, intentionally embracing purpose and the power of partnerships. This ultimately results in increased meaning and margin in life, as time is maximized on what matters most.

In today's world, countless individuals feel compelled to "do it all." Yet, this is simply unattainable; there are just not enough hours in each day. When goals are often left unmet, this can lead to frustration on the part of the person making the goals, as well as the individuals impacted by the attainment of them. In an age of abundant innovation and ample opportunities for burnout, we must intentionally face the truth of the matter . . . Although there will never be enough time to accomplish it all, we can ignite productivity, tackling what truly matters with excellence, by prioritizing purpose.

Rather than attempting to undertake any and every task that crosses our paths, how might our lives be altered if we prioritized purpose as a means of igniting productivity? There has never been a better time to "start with why" (Sinek, 2011). Below are some questions to ponder before beginning any new endeavor. These questions are designed to aid in the pursuit of prioritizing purpose:

- What is my why—or purpose—in life? Now is the time to refer back to and reiterate the mission statement you developed during your earlier reading in chapter two, which should directly align with your why . . .

  _____
  _____
  _____
  _____
  _____
  _____
  _____
  _____
  _____

- As you ponder the possibility of taking part in new opportunities that will require your time and energy, it is important to consider whether each new opportunity aligns with your why. For example, think of a potential new endeavor or "to-do" you could take part in. Does this new opportunity align with your why? If so, why is this the case?

  _____
  _____
  _____
  _____
  _____
  _____
  _____
  _____
  _____

- Along these same lines, is this opportunity truly important and worthwhile for you to pursue, or is it something you feel obligated to do?

  _____
  _____
  _____
  _____
  _____
  _____
  _____
  _____
  _____
  _____

- In the event that you determine this to be a truly and important and worthwhile opportunity to pursue, why is this the case? What specifically makes this new endeavor worthy of your time?

  _____
  _____
  _____
  _____
  _____
  _____
  _____
  _____
  _____

- Thinking back to the "Big Rocks" illustration discussed in chapter two, does this opportunity align with the "Big Rocks" in your life, or does this seem to be more representative of the smaller rocks—or even the tiny grains of sand?

  _____
  _____
  _____
  _____
  _____

_____
_____
_____
_____

Cultivating the Maximizer Mindset entails putting our passions first. This will prevent us from becoming sidetracked too often by items that are important but not purpose-driven pursuits. This also requires being able to say no to the lesser "to-do" items in order to focus on mission-critical endeavors.

- Take a moment to ponder at least one opportunity on the horizon that is not related to your why . . . List this opportunity below:

_____
_____
_____
_____

- If you said no to pursuing this opportunity, take a moment to imagine the worst-case scenario . . . What is the most terrifying occurrence that could take place as a result of your turning down this opportunity?

_____
_____
_____
_____
_____
_____
_____
_____
_____

- Now, take a moment to ponder an alternative situation . . . If you said no to pursuing this opportunity, imagine the best-case scenario . . . What purposes would you have time to prioritize that otherwise might not be possible to pursue?

_____
_____
_____
_____
_____
_____
_____
_____
_____
_____
_____

Once we have determined our "Big Rocks" in accordance with our why, we can begin to lay out a plan of action, or to determine the "how." As Sinek (2011) states,

Once you know WHY you do what you do, the question is HOW will you do it? HOWs are your values or principles that guide HOW to bring your cause to life . . . It's the discipline to never veer from your cause, to hold yourself accountable to HOW you do things; that's the hardest part (p. 66).

• Take a moment to list at least three hows regarding one of the whys you mentioned above. In other words, how exactly will you go about accomplishing the purpose you have decided to prioritize?

1. _____
_____
_____
_____

2. _____
_____
_____
_____

3. _____
_____
_____

_____

_____

• Who will you enlist to support you in accomplishing these hows?

_____

_____

_____

_____

• When will you reach out to them?

_____

_____

_____

_____

• What roles will they take on in this process?

_____

_____

_____

_____

As we think of the possibility of enlisting others in pursuit of our purposes, we should also consider how we can support others in accomplishing their purposes. Those who maintain the Maximizer Mindset seek out ways to serve those within their spheres of influence, rather than simply seeking to be served.

For those who wholeheartedly desire to live as givers rather than takers, a number of steps were previously discussed in chapter six through which to achieve this goal. This way of living naturally results in healthier relationships, greater joy, and higher achievement at work.

1. Five-minute favors: What small favors can you help someone accomplish in five minutes or less in the coming week?

_____

_____

_____

_____

_____

_____

2. Ask for help: Who can you ask to help you by sharing a word of advice? How might this enable them to feel fulfilled along the way?

_____

_____

_____

_____

_____

_____

3. Specialize in acts of service: What are at least three ways at which you excel in supporting others? How might you use these gifts to help and encourage at least one person this coming week?

_____

_____

_____

_____

_____

_____

_____

_____

Focusing upon treating others as we want to be treated—thus imparting value to other's lives—will also add value to our own lives. In our fast-paced, frantic world, the goal of living out a joyful and productive life requires intentionality. Purpose and planning form the foundation of the Maximizer Mindset.

As John Maxwell wisely remarked, "People who add value to others do so intentionally. I say that because to add value, leaders must give of themselves, and that rarely occurs by accident." Cultivating the Maximizer Mindset requires intentional purpose, planning, and reflection. As we seek to add value to others' lives through treasuring truth to find freedom, prioritizing purpose to ignite productivity, and cultivating creativity by leveraging connections, we empower ourselves and others to work less, achieve more, and spread joy throughout each day.

REFERENCES

Sinek, S. (2011). *Start with why*. Harlow, England: Penguin Books.

About the Authors

Katie Alaniz, EdD, is a faculty member within the College of Education Behavioral Sciences at Houston Baptist University, where she also serves as director of the Center for Learning Innovations and Teaching Excellence (C-LITE). As a teacher and digital learning specialist for over a decade in both public and private schools, including her service as a digital learning specialist at River Oaks Baptist School, Dr. Alaniz guides educators as they meaningfully integrate digital tools and resources within their classrooms. Dr. Alaniz has coauthored *Naturalizing Digital Immigrants: The Power of Collegial Coaching for Technology Integration*; *Digital Media in Today's Classrooms: The Potential for Meaningful Teaching, Learning, and Assessment*; and *Collegial Coaching: Mentoring for Knowledge and Skills That Transfer to Real-World Applications*. Additionally, she has published a number of academic articles and presented at a variety of educational conferences in the United States and abroad. Her primary research interests include digital learning, collegial coaching, and teacher education. Dr. Alaniz and her husband Steven reside in Houston and together enjoy serving their community through a nonprofit outreach program called Apartment Life.

David Q. Hao, MA, JD, is a recovering attorney turned student success champion. He currently serves as the head of School at Veritas Christian Academy, an independent K–8 innovative classical school in Houston, Texas. Previously, David worked in higher education as the associate vice president of student affairs at the University of St. Thomas (Texas), the dean of student success at Houston Baptist University, and has taught classes at the graduate and undergraduate levels. David earned his Doctor of Jurisprudence and Master of Higher Education Administration degrees from Boston College, his Bachelor of Business Administration degree from Baylor University, and is a licensed attorney in the great state of Texas. David and his wife Claire live in Sugar Land, Texas with their three wonderful and powerful daughters.

www.ingramcontent.com/pod-product-compliance
Lightning Source LLC
Chambersburg PA
CBHW020708270326
41928CB00005B/330